nce

John Adamson, born at Poltimore, Devon, studied at the universities of Edinburgh and Geneva. He worked for several short periods in the translation department of the Banque Française du Commerce Extérieur in Paris and for eight months at the Berlitz School of Languages in London before embarking on a career in publishing, starting as a graduate trainee at Cambridge University Press. There he became European sales representative, later publicity manager and lastly export sales director, afterwards joining the National Portrait Gallery in London as head of publications and retailing. Since the early nineties he has been an independent publisher of books in the fine and decorative arts as well as a writer and translator. He was awarded a fellowship of the Society of Antiquaries in 2019.

Clive Jackson grew up in Colchester, Essex, where he attended Colchester Royal Grammar School. After working for a year in the overseas business department of a City of London insurance company, he studied for a University of London degree in French and Spanish. Deciding on a career as a modern language teacher, he lived abroad for a number of years teaching French in Canada and English in the south of France. Long resident in Cambridge, he worked in adult education as a Spanish tutor, completing his career as head of Spanish at the Perse School.

George Adamson: *Tuileries Gardens, Paris*, 1971

Footloose in France

John Adamson and Clive Jackson

John Adamson
Cambridge

British Library Cataloguing in Publication Data
A catalogue record for this book is available from the British Library.

Published by John Adamson, 90 Hertford Street, Cambridge
CB4 3AQ, England

First published in 2023
ISBN 978-1-898565-18-5
E-book: 978-1-898565-19-2

Designed by Chris Jones Design, London, and set in Minion Pro and Myriad Pro Condensed
Printed and bound in England by the Lavenham Press Ltd, Lavenham, Suffolk

Cover: *Saint-Jean-de-Luz*, oil on canvas, 1907,
Albert Marquet (1875–1947), State Hermitage Museum, St Petersburg.
© Bridgeman Images

Frontispiece: *Tuileries Gardens, Paris*, gouache, 1971,
George Worsley Adamson (1913–2005), private collection.
© Estate of George Worsley Adamson

Contents

Prologue

The estuary had been transformed. For once the high-tide waters were glistening under a late summer light. The murky, muddy water had become an almost smooth stretch of blue. Seen from the open sea, the beach seemed to be edged with shingle and seaweed against which wavelets were lazily breaking.

They both lay stretched out on one of the little wooden floating platforms anchored an easy swim away from the beach, feeling as if they were bobbing on a small raft. Gently rocked by the waves, Clive closed his eyes and imagined he had been whisked away to the French Atlantic coast. It was like so many other moments from another far-off era, but which had suddenly become as vivid as if it were yesterday. There was the same seaside ambience: that slight breeze that blew into your ears; a sense of being in a great sun-drenched place, of being out of doors, of everything being possible.

"You'd think it was the Mediterranean," said John, almost putting the words into Clive's mouth. "With this bright light, this warmth, surrounded by blue like this, I feel as though I am in France rather than England!"

"Yes!", Clive agreed. "I know it's not the Riviera, but at least it's like being at the beach somewhere in France. The Atlantic coast, perhaps. With that carefree feeling of youth, knowing you had your whole life ahead of you."

He was about to add: "Just like being at the beach at Saint-Jean-de-Luz," but John had already begun talking about a day he had spent at La Baule, a more northerly Atlantic seaside resort in the Loire-Atlantique, in the company of three French girls.

"That was the first time I had been in France, you know. I was sixteen years old. I was staying in the Loire-Atlantique with Hélène Saint-Maur at her small château (or so I liked to call it), together with her two nieces Anne and Michèle and their friend Françoise, who were spending the summer at her house. It was the three girls who had taken me to the seaside in Hélène's draughty Deux Chevaux car," he explained. "Friendship with the Saint-Maur family went far back. Long, long ago, my grandmother had been Hélène's governess and, when my grandmother died, my mother had kept up contact with the family, corresponding with Madame Saint-Maur, Hélène's mother and then with Hélène for many years. A very handy contact it turned out to be, when I wanted to enjoy the thrill of living in Paris."

Already Clive's own thoughts were turning towards his first experience of France – towards the south-west.

"Tell me a bit more about it," said Clive, just to be polite.

"Well, there was René, Hélène's younger brother who worked for an advertising agency in Paris." John took a deep breath.

But Clive, lulled by the lapping of the water against the raft, had his mind elsewhere. A picture of the sleepy small town of Salies – the first of several – came into his head and lingered there as John began to tell his tale.

1.
An Englishman in the ninth district

At long last the Calais train was trundling through the outskirts of the capital. After a dreary trek through the rather featureless flatlands of northern France I was half expecting to see from the carriage window a spectacular city with all the well-known sights I knew from postcards, but much to my disappointment, all I saw were rather shabby dwellings and bare concrete walls stained with mould. Then, mercifully, as the train slowed down, the familiar shape of the basilica of the Sacré-Cœur came into view, standing out on the hill of Montmartre against a wan late August sky.

Within minutes, the train drew to a halt beneath the vast glazed roof of the Gare du Nord. It was peak rush hour, and René Saint-Maur, a slim, bespectacled, middle-aged man with moustache, was there on the platform to meet me, standing tall amongst the thronging crowd. He was holding up a photograph of me and checking it against the passengers who were climbing down the steps from the train.

"Hello, John," he said with almost the cut-glass accent of an English army officer, as he shook my hand, "Welcome to Paris!"

To start with, he insisted on speaking to me in English. That way, he must have supposed, I would not feel too out of place on this, my first visit to the French capital.

We made straight for a *brasserie* on the station to slake the thirst of the parched traveller. Everything seemed so utterly

French. The smartly aproned *garçons*, nimble-footed and nimble-tongued, were quick to throw in their shrewd remarks to add to the deep and earnest discussions going on all around us. But what horrible gassy beer they were serving on tap!

René in a very business-like way handed me back the photograph, lent me his copy of *Paris par arrondissement*, a pocket-sized book of maps of Paris, district by district with street index – and slipped a fifty-franc note into my hand. As we sipped our beers, he told me where I might stay for a few days and gave me some tips on what I should do about finding myself a summer job. We then walked swiftly out of the station, climbed into a taxi and were soon swept along in the never-ending stream of traffic down the boulevard de Magenta.

Before long, we were in a maze of narrow streets, where suddenly the Art-Déco frontage of the Folies-Bergère theatre caught my eye. The taxi turned into the rue de Trévise and stopped outside a large doorway above which were the initials U.C.J.G. in capital letters.

"Here's the hostel," explained René. "Let me introduce you to the secretary general . . ."

So, this was the Union Chrétienne de Jeunes Gens, or in other words the Paris YMCA! It was a rather drab, turn-of-the-century building, with interior decoration in a tired 1950s style, yet still with architectural features that spoke of a former glory. It was then, for the first time, that I began to feel far from home.

René left me to check in at the reception desk and told me to come and see him the next morning at his office at Richard Nelkène Publicité, an advertising agency on the quai de Grenelle near the Bir-Hakeim Grenelle Métro station.

After I had filled in the official registration form and made myself at home in the room I was to share with another guest, I took my first stroll in Paris. Down the entrance steps of the UCJG I went and turned left to find myself, within hardly more than a few strides, surrounded by the beautiful tall white houses of the Cité Bergère; then a few steps further and I was on the rue du Faubourg-Montmartre. There I saw the biggest crowd I had ever seen. Far from the narrow Devon lanes with their high hedgerows, here I was now in a bustling street with multi-storied buildings rising high on each side as I was borne along by the crowd past countless eating and drinking houses until I reached the Brébant strategically sited at the junction with the boulevards Montmartre and Poissonnière. This was the largest café in the neighbourhood, and there, on its terrace overflowing onto the pavement, people were chatting animatedly in the late summer evening twilight.

With a big ice cream in my hand, I continued my walk, wondering how I was going to fit into this very different world.

2.
Clive's voyage into the unknown

January was hanging heavily upon us, our mood for once subdued, but we knew that as soon as our well-liked French lecturer came into the lecture theatre where we students were gathered, the grey of this cheerless London winter morning would vanish. For us, Mr Matthews was most certainly in the first division as far as charisma and the quality of his lectures were concerned. With his relaxed teaching style punctuated with some joke or other he would instruct and entertain us in such an engaging way that our interest never wavered.

Suddenly, out of the corner of my eye I spotted a streak of scarlet. The room fell silent and there was Mr Matthews in front of us on the podium, putting his notes down on the lectern. Always elegantly attired, with a flamboyant line in neckwear, today he was sporting a red silk tie. We felt better already, the gloomy London weather forgotten.

"Is there anybody here who would be interested in living in France for a year?" he announced.

We certainly had not been expecting that. To go and live in France, a country whose language we were beginning to know better but of whose lifestyle we knew precious little. Was he taking us for a ride? I did not think so, but what could all this mean?

"Do you mean that we'd be off on a twelve-month holiday?" asked some joker from the back of the class.

"No chance of that," replied Mr Matthews with a smile. "Let

me explain to you what this involves, for this is actually a brand-new opportunity for you as students of French to improve your knowledge of the language. You will get the chance to work as English-language assistants in secondary schools in various parts of the country."

With his characteristic enthusiasm, he continued to explain to us that we would be contracted to teach for twelve hours a week and that we would receive a modest remuneration from the French ministry of education for our work. It goes without saying that the whole idea seemed enormously attractive to us. You can just imagine our excitement at the prospect of a year of freedom in a foreign land, and, what is more, for which we would be paid! Judging by the scrum of eager students surrounding Mr Matthews at the end of the lecture it was clear that there would be no shortage of volunteers.

When we submitted our applications, we also had to state the preferred region we would like to go to. In my case, I had asked for a town within easy reach of Spain, for I hoped to nip over the border and keep up my Spanish as well. A reply from the French authorities was not long in coming. I had struck lucky! I had been allocated to a secondary school in Salies-de-Béarn. A quick look at the map showed me that Salies was in the deep south-west of France, midway between Bayonne and Pau, and only a short distance from Spain.

I soon found out where some of the others were going. Dave from Devon was delighted that he would soon be off to Brittany, and I was very glad to learn that my close friend Peter had landed himself a posting to the town of Montréjeau in the Haute-Garonne, for when I took another look at the map, I saw that he was going to be even nearer to the Pyrenees than I would be and therefore not so very far away at all.

3.
René

Opéra; Madeleine; Concorde; Invalides. My first ever ride on the Métro had begun, taking me towards René's office on the quai de Grenelle. I had bought my first *carnet*, a wad of ten second-class tickets at the Rue Montmartre station and was amused to be passing some of the familiar landmarks of Paris, but underground. I had not yet seen any of these sites at street level.

At that time Dubonnet had an extensive advertising campaign underway for its aperitif with the slogan "Dubo . . . Dubon . . . Dubonnet". Just as the train came into some of the stations along the way this slogan was painted in big black letters on the murky tunnel wall, so that just as you approached the station and the growing light the words flashed by the train window: dimly you could make out the first word: DUBO; then more clearly DUBON; and then more clearly still the whole word DUBONNET. And all that happened before reaching the bright lighting of the station itself. Which publicity agency had come up with this simple but clever idea and witty play on words?

My train was coming to a halt at La Motte-Picquet station. There I had to change from underground to elevated railway in the direction of Étoile. Now the train ran in the broad light of day between the smart apartment blocks of the Grenelle district and dropped me off two stops away at Bir-Hakeim Grenelle, a stone's throw from the Eiffel Tower.

It was easy enough finding the right building, but who would have believed that what looked like little more than a cupboard door was the way into the offices of Richard Nelkène Publicité, a well-established advertising agency? I asked for Monsieur Saint-Maur and was shown to his office. What a huge man he seemed to be, perched behind his desk; and as he rose to shake my hand, even taller than he had seemed only yesterday. He was delighted to receive the gift of a set of Dartington glass goblets I had brought him from my parents.

"Now, let's see what we can do about finding you a temporary job in Paris." He seemed as determined as I was to find me something and started by ringing round a few contacts. The calls all began with an authoritative "Bonjour . . . C'est René Saint-Maur à l'appareil."

How puzzling. What could the end of this phrase mean? Was it something to do with "rendre la pareille", or returning a favour, but no: it soon became clear that this was the expression the French used when identifying themselves on the telephone. "Good morning. It's René Saint-Maur speaking."

We then strolled round to the CIDJ, a student agency in its brand-new wooden office near the Eiffel Tower, where, after a wearisome wait, the girl at the desk came up with only one job suggestion which René did not think would be any good for me anyway. Back at the office, he made an appointment for me that afternoon with COPAR, another acronym, another student agency; and then he had a brainwave. He rang the British Embassy.

"A Miss Rodman is expecting you at the embassy this afternoon," he said, hanging up. "You have nothing to lose, you know: every now and again, businesses ask the embassy if it knows of any local native English speaker for some small short-term job or other. It's well worth a try, 'anyhaa'." He often ended his sentences with this adverb, uttered with what sounded like a rather aristocratic English accent.

By then it was time for lunch, but first we had a quick drink in his office: a Tomatin whisky (his favourite malt) with a squirt of soda.

Sitting on the terrace of a nearby restaurant along the banks of the Seine with a senior executive from a top advertising agency was the height of sophistication for a 19-year-old English student on his first ever full day in Paris. Looking up from my *omelette au jambon* the lofty girders of the combined elevated-railway and road bridge spanning the river filled my field of vision with the mechanical wonders of a great metropolis. High up, along the viaduct, a green Métro train clattered slowly towards Passy on the opposite bank and halted briefly at the station before vanishing into a tunnel; far below, a barge floated sedately past the long islet in the Seine known as the allée des Cygnes or Path of Swans. But a few hundred yards away, towering over everything in all its sweeping ironwork glory was another outstanding feat of engineering, one designed by Gustave Eiffel's company for the Universal Exhibition of 1889.

"One way or another, we'll find you a job," René said as he finished his *express* and raised his other hand for the bill.

But finding employment, even short-term, for a young foreigner without any work experience was not easy. I went to see COPAR over in the Latin Quarter as planned, but they were unable to help me, and then, trailing all the way across town on foot, arrived at the British Embassy just before it shut for the weekend.

The rue du Faubourg Saint-Honoré was truly the epitome of chic and diplomacy. Looking back down the rue Boissy d'Anglas between the bulk of the Hôtel de Crillon on one side and that of the American Embassy on the other was a far-off glimpse of the place de la Concorde I had just skirted . . . I turned left and almost before I knew where I was there rose up the great carriage entrance of my embassy at number 35. Further along the street a blue-and-white sign with a small arrow pointed to the nearby

Anglican church of Saint Michael in the rue d'Aguesseau opposite, but high up on the wall, right above where I stood, was a much grander and more imposing nameplate in gold and silver on which were inscribed the words, "Her Britannic Majesty's Embassy" and beneath them the enigmatic word "CHANCERY".

I hesitated at the entrance for a moment or two, then, overcoming my reservations, eased open the little door set in the big one and there under the porchway found a small glass-windowed security office.

Once I had explained the purpose of my visit, I was taken into the magnificent, marbled hallway of the main building, where the receptionist said Miss Rodman was out but that I should fill in a form anyway. She said Miss Rodman would see me on Monday morning.

Monday, I was back at the embassy sitting in the hallway waiting for Miss Rodman to come down from one of the offices upstairs to answer my job enquiry. How charming and welcoming she was, and so very English, as she ushered me into a luxurious office on the ground floor overlooking an Italianate garden.

"Please don't think that this is my office," she said seating herself at a small desk. "But do have a seat."

Once I was comfortably ensconced, she went on to explain how every now and again the embassy was told by potential employers of job opportunities for Britons living in the city. But this came with a word of caution: demand was always unpredictable.

"As it happens, we've just had a request in from an English gentleman who works in an international bank here in Paris," she said. "He's looking for someone who could fill in for him as head of translation when he goes on holiday later this month. Would that be of interest to you?"

I could hardly believe my own ears. But the scrap of paper on which she had written: "Ronald Buckley, Banque Française du

Commerce Extérieur, 21 Boulevard Hausmann" was safely tucked away in my pocket as I left the embassy.

After a light lunch near the Madeleine, I went back to see René, who let me use his office phone to ring Mr Buckley at the bank. But Mr Buckley had just a few hours before taken on someone else for the job. Oh! I had been so near and yet so far.

Undeterred, René came up with other suggestions to try the next day: two grander, international acronyms sprang to mind: UNESCO and OECD; and, if no luck at the British Embassy, why not try the American Embassy too? Filled with renewed hope, I left him to prepare for his imminent two-day trip to Madrid and London on a sales campaign to promote Lipton's tea.

"On se téléphone," were his parting words in French, "Let's speak on the phone."

4.
Clive the grape-picker

My journey to the south-west started in mid-September, not in the company of Peter but of Ian, another student on my course, who was heading to France to work for a year at a secondary school in the Cévennes. There was, however, something else we were keen to do before embarking on our teaching "careers". Ian had learnt from a friend of his, who had worked there the year before, that a prestigious château in the Bordeaux wine district was looking for pickers to help with the grape harvest. Always game for a new challenge, I agreed to sign up, like him, for the duration of the harvest at Château Beauregard, one of the great producers of red wine in the Pomerol.

After the boat train from London, we took the night express from the Gare d'Austerlitz in Paris down towards the south-west. We did not know that we could have booked a sleeping-berth, so found ourselves sitting up all night in an ordinary train compartment. That was no great hardship, for, more likely than not, the novelty of the journey would have kept us wide awake anyway. As the train hurtled along, the train inspector marched up and down the carriage corridors and repeated, mantra-like, the name of each station at which we would soon be stopping: "Prochain arrêt Orléans, next stop Orléans!" And afterwards in their turn: Tours; Poitiers; Angoulême.

We had no concept of the vast distances between each of those stations, but then, suddenly, at the first glimmering of dawn, we heard him announce "Bordeaux Saint-Jean", where we were to alight. There were still two hours to wait before the next train would take us to Libourne, the nearest station to the château. Enough time to enjoy a relaxed breakfast.

Opposite the station we spotted a café where the waiters had already started their morning shift. Just as we were leaving the station, we caught sight of two middle-aged ladies, both heavily painted in make-up, who were slouching provocatively against the wall. They seemed to be scanning all the passengers as they came out of the station building, but it was us whom they fixed with a gimlet stare as they shouted out:

"Hey, you two boys look a bit tired; what about coming back to our place for a lie-down?"

Fortunately, they did not repeat the offer as we scuttled past them and crossed the road for the far more appealing temptation of coffee and croissants.

From Libourne, some hours later we reached the château at last by taxi and found ourselves in the midst of a crowd of other young workers. They were all students, most of them French, but we soon learnt there were also three Belgians and two Dutch amongst them. After the owner of the château had come out to greet us and brief us on the work we would be undertaking, he led us to a string of cottages that were to be our home throughout the harvest.

Next morning the estate foremen went with us to the vineyard to get us started. I stood there gazing at row upon row of vines which seemed to stretch to infinity, each vine laden with its bunches of dark grapes basking in the early morning sunlight. And so, the harvest began. At first, the work did not seem too arduous. Clutching our secateurs and with our baskets slung before us, we stooped in front of each vine and carefully snipped off its bunches of exquisite fruit. What a pastoral dream! Yet, as time wore on, the sun climbed higher in the sky, the shadows grew shorter, our shirts began to stick to our backs, the relentless squeezing with our fingers began to make them hurt, and the growing burden of the picked grapes began to weigh us down. When the baskets were full, we would empty the bunches of grapes into one of the awaiting trailers that then took away the fruit to be crushed and fermented. But when on earth would we be stopping for a break? Gradually the notion of having a rest merged with that of having something to eat. Gurgling behind the now heavy weight on my stomach was a very empty belly.

To my great relief, at half past twelve we were told to lay down our baskets, for lunch was now ready. For the duration of the grape harvest the weather remained hot and sunny and so every day we were able to dine outdoors sitting on forms at long tables. There was never a lull in the conversation, and although we usually chatted in French, every now and again there were always a few who fancied practising their English.

Our employers did more than look after our culinary well-being at lunchtime, for every evening there was a twilight dinner washed down with plenty of wine, followed by dancing in one of the grand rooms of the château, with all the armchairs pushed back against the walls. What a contrast to the heaving dance floor of the Whisky à Gogo club in London where I spent many a Saturday night!

It was at the dance on the third evening that I noticed her, a young woman standing slightly away from the dancing area. Even in the dimly lit room I could see that she was strikingly attractive. With her blue eyes and her fair hair braided round her head, could she have come from the north of France rather than from the south? Hers was a kind of beauty to which I have always been susceptible. Despite feeling a little apprehensive, I plucked up enough courage to walk the few steps over to her. She turned towards me and when she heard my first faltering words of French spoken with a slight English accent began to smile. It seemed no time at all before we were happily chatting away, at ease in each other's company.

Marianne was from Bordeaux, but she told me that she was studying at Toulouse University. She said her family had moved down from Alsace in the north-east of France. She was the first French girl I had ever met, and I found her fascinating! It was not just because she was French – there was more to it than that. I hoped this would not be just a fleeting encounter, for I had soon realized that I wanted us to meet up again.

My knowledge of French geography was limited, admittedly, but it struck me there and then that if our friendship were to bloom, travelling the distance between Salies, where I would be working, and Toulouse, where she was studying, would not be too long a journey and one that I would be more than eager to undertake.

Next day, back among the vines, I looked around straining my eyes to see if I could spot her slender figure. To no avail; she must have been working in another team some way off, or perhaps even picking grapes at another château.

Time was running out. The grape-picking at my château was due to finish in five days' time and no doubt it would be about the same for her even if she was working on another estate. All the same, I hoped that she would turn up at the dance that evening.

When evening came, I tried to look my very best in jacket and jeans and made quite sure I was at the dance in good time. The room was full of my new-found acquaintances, some of whom seemed slightly puzzled that tonight I was neither especially keen to strike up conversation with them, nor take to the dance floor. Instead, I leant against the wall watching everybody come and go. While the records of Johnny Hallyday, Claude François and Françoise Hardy were being played at full blast, I just stood there anxiously waiting.

At long last, the door swung open and there before my eyes was Marianne, the picture of elegance in a dark-blue dress. I rushed over to greet her.

I said: "Do you like dancing as much as I do?"

She nodded, took my hand and led me onto the dance floor.

What a good thing it was that there were still a few remaining dancing evenings for us to get to know each other better. I was not looking forward to when they would come to an end.

When the owner turned up at the beginning of the last evening to thank us and pay our wages, it brought home to me that this really was the end of our grape-picking adventure. Sitting at a small desk, he called us over one by one to reward us for our labours and handed each of us a fistful of banknotes as well as a vintage bottle from his cellar. Judging by the way he was slurring his words he must surely have been sampling some of his own produce!

It was time to leave, and the young harvesters were wishing each other well before they headed back to autumn term at university. Ian was in high spirits as he set off for the Cévennes; my own journey down to the Béarn was much shorter than his, but as I left, I did feel rather low at the thought that I might never see Marianne again.

5.
John's stroll through Paris

From my very first weekend in Paris, the Tuileries Gardens became one of my haunts. It was hard to believe how relaxing it was to sit in a vast French garden like this in the middle of some of the busiest traffic in Europe. You knew the cars were there, you could just see them and hear them, but somehow, they did not command attention and the trees and gravelled glades made you forget them altogether. To reach the gardens from the hostel, I could either follow the main boulevards as far as the Madeleine church, amble down the rue Royale and go into the gardens from the place de la Concorde, or else I could strike south along what I thought was a much more interesting way: I would cross over the boulevard Montmartre then, after a ten-minute walk down the rue Vivienne, pass by the Bourse, Paris's stock exchange, and then, a few hundred yards further on, go down a few steps and take the passageway past the elegant windows of the Grand Véfour restaurant. And there before me was another much smaller rather formal garden belonging to the Palais-Royal.

A plaque at first-floor level reminded me each time I went by that the writer Colette had lived in a flat overlooking these neatly trimmed avenues of trees in the garden surrounded by arcaded walkways. But in her day, those same trees cannot have been much taller than shrubs! I would then stroll under the arcades to the Comédie-Française theatre, where, as my linguistic confidence grew, I was later to see performances of Molière's *Don Juan*, Jean

Giraudoux's *Ondine*, and Robert Hirsch playing Richard III in a French-language production directed by Terry Hands of the Royal Shakespeare Company. I would then cross the rue de Rivoli near the Palais-Royal Métro station and go into the main courtyard of the Louvre palace, where the Tuileries palace had once stood overlooking its elegant gardens laid out by Le Nôtre, which still stretched as far as the Concorde square.

Whenever I took this route, in those early days, I was always mobbed by photographers who were falling over themselves to take a picture of me, with, as backdrop, the Louvre or that broad chalk-white walkway which went up to the Concorde and seemed to stretch beyond – as far as the Arc de Triomphe.

Oh! Those pushy touts, who were frantically waving their hulking Polaroid cameras in the air for ever set on snapping every passing tourist, they were like a military phalanx. How on earth could I get through them without being pestered? Without having my photograph forcibly taken and a polaroid print developed before my eyes and thrust at me?

Seen from the magnificent gardens of the Tuileries the Louvre did look most imposing. One of the street photographers had well and truly got it into his head that it would look even better with my standing there before it and insisted on taking my photograph for twenty francs. I told him it was too much. His face dropped, and so did the price. It was still too much; then the price went down further to ten francs, at which point I pretended I had not the money and left the man, my unwanted Polaroid portrait still developing in his outstretched hand.

While Paris was still new to me, I found it impossible to hide the fact that I was a tourist. However, later, when I was working there, I wanted above all else to blend in with the rest of the community. I was faced with the challenge shared by everyone living abroad, namely: how do you become integrated in your host country without being assimilated? I had no intention whatsoever of denying either my country of origin or nationality but wished to reach a stage when I would be completely at home both culturally and linguistically if this were to become my adopted country. I set myself a goal. When eventually I could walk through the wall of photographers without being harassed as an unsuspecting tourist, then I knew for sure that I had succeeded.

*

On my first ever Saturday in Paris, I was strolling in the Tuileries Gardens not far from the place de la Concorde when I spotted to one side of the broad walkway a small crowd gathered round a youngish man with a striking profile who was very busy with what he was doing. Curiosity got the better of me and I edged closer. At last, I could see what was happening. He was standing there, holding a pair of scissors in his right hand and a sheet of black paper in his left. With swift and precise movements, he was cutting the paper to make a silhouette of the lady standing before him whom he eyed intensely. He cut round the shapes of her profile, a noble brow, a retroussé nose; he sketched in her lips, nose, blouse collar with accurate snips; he cut graceful curves of light out of the black paper to give greater volume to her hair. This little scene was unfolding before our eyes as he held us all spellbound. In less than no time the silhouette was done; it was beautiful; evocative. The lady was delighted and gladly handed over a few coins.

"Who's next," shouted the scissor man. "Come on now," I heard him say, as he bent his gaze towards me. "Come along."

I had been so impressed with what he had just done that I could not stop myself from stepping forward. For a few brief minutes I was the centre of attraction with tourists snapping away while he snipped. As skilful as ever, the man cut out a profile of my head, giving me eyelashes, a straight nose, and a neat hairstyle.

"Are you from Germany?" he asked.

I told him where I was from to which he responded with a few witty remarks even as he worked. The silhouette took shape as if by magic, the paper clippings falling away from his scissors. And lo and behold, the picture was complete.

Overjoyed, I paid up.

"Merci, au revoir l'Angleterre!" said the man as I took my silhouette. What I saw before me was recognizable at once, but my image had been refined in a rather French way, and what I saw was a version of myself that I had not yet become.

*

On the boat train I had read in *The Times* that there was to be a solemn vigil that evening at the Hôtel de Ville as part of the ceremonies to mark the liberation of Paris twenty-five years ago. So, after dinner at the youth hostel, I walked over there, hoping that I was still in time.

The great square before the town hall was thronged with people and soldiers – and tanks. How moving it was to stand in a French crowd and witness their pride and patriotism. A flame was burning in a great metallic basin outside the portals of the town hall and standing in the square a military band was playing lively, stirring tunes. Then, over loudspeakers came the announcement that the hall would be illuminated after a minute's silence and further music.

Suddenly, at just after eleven o'clock, all the church bells of Paris began to peal as they had done twenty-five years before; and, as the Hôtel de Ville was lit up dramatically in a kind of *son et lumière*, the pigeons huddled on their stony perches flew away in fright, their flapping wings caught fleetingly in the shifting beams of light. More and more fireworks were lit from the top of the town hall. First there was a great luminous glow as rockets formed a tricolour in the black night sky. Then came bangers and more rockets which rounded off the celebration of Paris's liberation in bursts of sound and light. And for many of the Parisians standing in the square all of this brought back tearful memories of that extraordinary moment in the history of their city.

*

My first visit to Paris would not have been complete without a visit to the cathedral of Notre-Dame. Armed with my newly acquired green Michelin guide (I had opted for the French edition so as not to seem too much like a foreign visitor) I walked around its vast nave, which was bathed in a light of many colours streaming down from the stained-glass windows; and then, to crown my experience, I bought myself a ticket to climb the winding stairs up to the tower gallery. From the parapet, Paris was spread out before me. I was delighted to look down at the Seine as it snaked its way into the distance; the Eiffel tower was etched against the skyline dwarfing a sea of buildings roofed in zinc and slate. In the middle distance loomed the hulk of the Louvre palace with its steep mansarded roof, and beyond that, there lay my favourite route leading towards the Concorde and the Champs-Élysées. Turning my gaze northwards, I could make out more familiar landmarks: the hill of Montmartre; the Trinité church below it and the Madeleine nearer still. Somewhere in this maze of streets and alleyways was the hostel where I was staying. I felt as though I was living at the heart of a very big village.

Yet, up there on the gallery, besides a few other energetic sightseers, I found myself sharing the view with a number of neo-Gothic creatures of fantasy and mythology carved in stone. With the wind whistling around them, theirs was an inscrutable weather-beaten gaze: it was as if they were taking everything in without anybody being aware.

I just had to go back to Notre-Dame some days later: I wanted to see what it was like during a Sunday mass. On my way there from the UCJG I found myself walking through a lively bird market. The birds were in full chorus: from the aisles of stacked cages came not just the chitter-chatter of budgerigars and the squawks of parakeets but the cooing of doves and the melodious chirrups and warbles of songbirds as well.

As I entered the basilica a priest in a sumptuous green chasuble was blessing the assembled and bidding them go forth.

A mass was coming to an end, so presently I was able to find a vacated rush-bottomed chair not too far from the altar. The church was now milling with pilgrims and tourists. Then, without warning, the great organ began to play, soon drowning all other sounds in eerie discordant outbursts, in fanfares and deep growls.

By the time the rite started half an hour later, with the bishop, priests and deacons, followed by acolytes in their cassocks and cottas, solemnly processing to the altar, every seat had been taken. Disconcertingly, there were frequent flashes from cameras from all around the nave. Part way through the mass a fiery sermon held the congregation's rapt attention for a whole quarter of an hour . . .

All in all, it had been an uplifting experience on a magnificent scale. Beams of sunlight slanting down from the great rose window in a burst of bright colours fell now onto the chequered transept floor, and, for a fleeting moment, onto the veils and bare heads of those worshippers near the altar as slowly they began to rise to their feet and wend their way towards the Great West Door. And yet, as I shuffled with the crowd, I once again shuddered inwardly with that unsettling feeling that those stony chimeras up there on the tower gallery had given me as they watched over the cityscape from aloft.

I had taken a black-and-white photograph of one of the statues with the whole of the sixth and seventh districts stretching out beneath it. And when I got back to England, I made it into a linocut, carefully cutting out its profile and working my way round the grotesque curves with my gouge.

John Adamson: *View from the Tower Gallery, Notre-Dame, Paris,* c. 1970. © John Adamson

6.
Clive arrives at Salies-de-Béarn

Reaching an unknown destination often comes hand in hand with a slight feeling of unease: even more so when you know that you are about to spend a year of your life there. The exoticism of this country and its ways so different from those in England were already making me feel even more like a foreigner. I began to wonder if I would be able to fend for myself so far from my roots. I could only hope that I would be able to take up the challenge. Looking out of the carriage window at the immense tracts of open countryside I did my best to banish my misgivings. As my train neared Puyoô, where I had to alight for Salies-de-Béarn, my mind was in a whirl. What would life be like in such a remote place as this?

I left the station precinct at Puyoô in a taxi, my bulging suitcase in the boot. Salies was only minutes away and as we neared the town, what a tiny place this was! Looking out of the taxi window I saw that there were not many people out and about. We drove along narrow deserted streets lined with terraced houses, many of which had an old-fashioned charm about them. Some had their shutters closed even though it was the middle of the day. As we went along, my fears were dominated by one niggling thought: used as I was to the cosmopolitan life of London, how on earth was I going to adapt to life in this backwater?

The taxi slowed down. I saw that we were nearing an austere-looking building dominating a small square.

"Here we are then, Monsieur, there's the school. Do you need a receipt?"

In the all-pervading stillness of the mid-afternoon heat, I walked into the courtyard. All you could hear were the droning voices of teachers as they gave their lessons.

I put down my case and knocked on the headmaster's office door. His secretary opened it.

"Good afternoon, Madame, er, I am the new English language assistant."

"Ah, yes, of course. We have been expecting you. It's Mr Jackson, isn't it? Welcome to the school."

Standing there in her neat outfit she gave off an air of efficiency, and professionalism, and yet could not quite disguise the fact that she was slightly taken aback. Instead of the English stereotype, she beheld a tall, 21-year-old, sun-tanned man in short sleeves and jeans, with a somewhat Mediterranean look – and green eyes.

She went off to find Monsieur Clavère, the headmaster, who then came to the door and invited me in.

"Do sit down," he said, shaking me by the hand.

A man of medium build in his late fifties, he had a solemn air about him, his neat sartorial appearance in keeping with his professional status. As we chatted, I tried to hide my nervousness, for I could feel the gulf between us in terms of years and experience. We must have spent a full quarter of an hour discussing in depth the teaching methods employed in France and how they would apply to my new job as language assistant.

Finally, he came around to the matter of my lodgings, something that I had been wondering about.

He told me that the school boarding-house was on the edge of town. Across the way from it, he said, was a much smaller house which I would be sharing with three French teaching colleagues. However, they were only there during the working week since their own family homes were too far away for them to make the daily journey to work.

I set off from the school and found that it took me a good ten minutes to get to my accommodation, by which time I was exhausted by the long uphill climb, and my suitcase had felt heavier and heavier.

Upon arrival at the house, the last thing I was expecting was for there to be a reception committee. But there outside the front door stood three young men. One of them came over to greet me.

"Well now! Here's our Englishman who has arrived at last! By the way, I'm René."

He was wearing horn-rimmed glasses and beaming at me in a warm and mischievous way. I clicked straightaway that this young gentleman must be the leader of the pack. The other two came over to say hello. Jean-Baptiste was a well-built young lad, whereas Joseph was tall and lanky. I felt like the young d'Artagnan arriving to join up with his gang of Gascon musketeers.

This first encounter stood out in my mind for the spontaneous warmth of their welcome. These three young fellows, each with his own personality: René the extrovert; Joseph more self-contained; and Jean-Baptiste, with that natural Basque reserve. Little did I know at that time what extraordinary ties of friendship would form between us over the coming months.

From the outside, our residence was anything but impressive; on the contrary, it was rather run down and sad looking. On the other hand, the boarding-house opposite had once been quite a fine mansion house set in its own small park and it still retained its estate name of "Mosquéros".

Once over the threshold of our residence, the look of the interior was scarcely better than the outside. We climbed up to the first floor, where I was shown my room. It was sparsely furnished: there was an iron bed; a cupboard in which hung misshapen coat hangers; and on the bare oaken floorboards there was not a rug to be seen. At least there was one good thing: the bed-linen, I was told, was laundered free of charge.

I had barely had time to empty out my suitcase and put away my clothes in the cupboard when René knocked on the door and told me dinner was ready. Not for us the task of having to prepare our own evening meals; all of us teachers were catered for in a dining-room of our own next to the pupils' canteen at the boarding-house.

The admirable Madame Lagourgue was in charge of cooking there, and she was the lady who worked tirelessly to make sure we were properly fed. For our part, we never failed to do justice to her gastronomic creations. Such a contrast to those dreadful stews in England made from gristly and fatty meat, which were thrust at us as school dinners! What is more, how delightful it was to find that bottles of red wine were put on the table for us teachers.

At table, mealtimes were never silent affairs. Far from it.

Each of us, with René taking the lead, was always ready to express his own point of view at those dinner-table debates, which were so often of a political nature.

"Society must think in a way that is *populaire*," said René. "We really do have to offer opportunities to the working class; that's got to be the way forward."

At the outset, I struggled to follow these lively discussions where everyone was talking ten to the dozen. Sometimes, not infrequently, René would bring up the topic of Algeria's war of independence, about which I knew virtually nothing. René's older brother had been conscripted into the French army and had seen active service in Algeria, an experience, René said, that had deeply affected him.

It took me a few weeks to get into the swing of things, especially when it came to expressing myself in French. The Béarnais accent with its gutsy sound threw me. Hearing its highly articulated vowels it was a bit like French and its neighbouring language

Spanish on the other side of the Pyrenees rolled into one.

Luckily, before too long, I grew used to it. My confidence soared and after two months I found that I could follow more or less everything that was being said.

Whenever we went for a spin in René's car, it was fun listening to the strong accent of his stentorian speech that even drowned out the sound of the car's engine. He loved taking me to small bastide towns that had witnessed the advancing armies of the Middle Ages, when England ruled Aquitaine and found itself so often at war with France. In every town to which we came his enthusiasm for the history of the region was almost palpable: as the car slowed down, his speech speeded up, and sometimes he would round off a visit with a remark along the lines of:

"Just look at all these wonderful places Clive, can't you see what you English have lost!"

7.
John finds a job in the big city

From my very first evening at the UCJG, I got to know some of the other young residents and staff, either in the self-service dining-room, in the lobby with its easy chairs and stacks of magazines or in the small breakfast-room. And very quickly I realized that I was not the only one to have come from afar. For sure, most of the residents were either from provincial France or from a French-speaking country. There were all sorts of folk, mostly young men, from west and central Africa, from Tunisia and Morocco, but some also from Germany and Italy, all of them in Paris, whether for study or work, and in need of modestly priced accommodation. All of us needed to familiarize ourselves with the Parisian way of life, each in his own way. Even though the hostel was a rather mournful place, everybody without exception was kind, open-minded and welcoming. As for me, it was my first sustained encounter with the cosmopolitan world, my first real taste of other civilizations and other ways of life.

One of the first residents with whom I struck up a friendship was Georges, a young designer from Toulouse working in a film studio. Slightly built, handsome and open-faced, he had a ready smile.

No sooner had he found out I was English than he asked, struggling a bit with the words as he uttered with a strong French accent the tongue-twister name, "Tu aimes Creedence Clearwater Revival?"

*

I had alighted from the boat train at the Gare du Nord, my mind made up: I did not want to be a mere tourist in Paris or indeed just an earnest student trying to practise his French, but to be, albeit only for a short while, a worker, a part of the fabric of the city.

So, undaunted by my failure to secure that translating job at the French bank I thought time would be well served if I tried some of the other institutions René and I had agreed were worth contacting.

At the UNESCO building on the place Fontenoy in the seventh arrondissement I was quite taken aback to behold such a colossal piece of modern architecture laid out in what looked like three curving blades of a giant propeller. At reception I was given a little map with directions to the room of Miss Chase. What better name for the woman in charge of employment who was helping job-hunters like me! The scale of everything was so great that even with the map I felt rather lost. Conversations reverberated down corridors without end in a babble of languages.

At the OECD I found myself not far from the Bois de Boulogne in the grounds of a château-like building. This I soon learnt had been built for the baron de Rothschild in the 1920s, and there, in the late eighteenth century in what had been parkland around an earlier château, the first, manned, untethered flight by hot-air balloon had set off. Sadly, the romantic aura of Rothschild's château in its revival neo-classical style conjuring up a lost age of great individual wealth was marred by a modern annex structure recently built nearby that in its thoroughly utilitarian aspect was quite out of keeping with the earlier building and its setting.

I was ushered up a grand marble staircase, then into an old-fashioned lift that rattled slowly upwards – like a mature economy – to the administrative offices. But nothing came of my visit.

At the ORTF, a bold, modernist building in glass and concrete formed a giant ring around a central tower to house the newly consolidated headquarters for French state-owned broadcasting. Here there was an almost palpable buzz in the air as I stood in the lobby, but no job for me.

For all that job-hunting, I did not forget altogether about doing a little tourism, however, and punctuated my "business meetings" with some exhibitions: a blockbuster show at the Grand Palais marking the bicentenary of Napoleon's birth; and in contrast the fascinating permanent exhibition then on display at the Palais de la découverte in the avenue Franklin-Roosevelt that in the sequence of galleries taught the different laws of science in a way that was easy to understand.

Another visit to René was called for to keep him up to date. I felt certain that he would be tired of seeing me and of my taking up his valuable time. But no, when I found him at his desk at Richard Nelkène Publicité he was as friendly and encouraging as ever, albeit with little time to spare before heading out for an external appointment, but just enough to share his enthusiasm for his upcoming two-day campaign trip to London and Madrid to promote the sales of Lipton's tea.

"On se téléphone!"

With renewed determination I went on scouting for job opportunities. At the office for student jobs and accommodation on the rue Jean-Calvin over in the fifth arrondissement off the rue Mouffetard, I made use of René's surprising Anglicism:

"I am looking for 'un job' in Paris."

"Voulez-vous *une chambre* dans une résidence universitaire? Do you want a room in a students' hall of residence?" the young man behind the counter answered me with a query.

"A job!"

I was upset by this lack of understanding. How could I ever have thought that *chambre* was a masculine noun!

I made my way back a few days later to the quai de Grenelle to tell René the lack of news. His young colleague Acqua Vita in his dashing dark-blue double-breasted jacket joined us for lunch round the corner. There I had roast duck for the first time ever. It was quite delicious, and of course the company was excellent. I mentioned the fact that over the weekend I had been to see Serge Gainsbourg and Jane Birkin starring in the newly released film *Slogan*. Grimblat's new film lacked the charm of *Un homme et une femme* that I had seen with René's daughter and niece together with their friend Françoise in Nantes three years earlier. It did have some similar tragi-comical feelings though, and there was beautiful photography of Paris and Venice. Yet, somehow, it was more ordinary than Claude Lelouch's earlier film, redeeming itself a little nevertheless in the way it satirized the advertising world.

"I am not going to bother seeing the film," René declared. "I know exactly what happens in the advertising world."

Acqua Vita said he knew Jane Birkin, who had star billing as an English girl in the film. I am sure he found her accent in French as beguiling as I did.

It was now almost two weeks since I had come to Paris and in my hunt for a job, I had ended up going to so many offices all over town, filling in so many dreary application forms and speaking to so many pretty, well-groomed ladies at reception desks.

"So sorry," each of them said. "Désolée."

Now the time had come to make one last attempt, this time at the Franco-British school at the Cité universitaire down in the fourteenth district. When I got there, nobody was manning the information desk. By then, though, I had had enough, so I simply gave up and caught the Ligne de Sceaux back to Denfert-Rochereau and from there the ordinary Métro to Bir-Hakeim Grenelle to update René once more. I found him tired and hungry, hotfoot from his London and Madrid trip. I had already had a *tranche néopolitaine* as a snack standing on the Passy bridge but joined him and Acqua Vita now with his fiancée, an attractive fashion-magazine cover girl, for a coffee while they had their lunch. Notwithstanding my failure on the job front, I must own that I was rather enjoying all my interactions on the fringes of the Paris world of business. My hopes of a summer job in Paris for that year were dashed, but I had already glimpsed the city as it worked.

After one last telephone call on my behalf to *Le Figaro* from his office, René said, "John, it's time to forget about a job, don't you think? For your last few days in Paris, why not just be a tourist?"

Telephonic communication was not so easy for either of us, since I was always on the go, and working public telephones were few and far between. So, when not so many days after René's return from his trip he wanted to reach me, he resorted to sending a *lettre pneumatique* to me at the hostel. Would I, he asked, show an English girl, the secretary of his colleague in London, around Paris? What a thoughtful idea of his this was: I could be a tourist in what I felt certain would prove to be good company.

But reaching René to make the necessary arrangements was again a challenge, for I had again to find a public telephone in working order; and then contact Jennifer. It was not until the next day, however, that I could reach her at her hotel from one of the telephone booths in the UCJG that took *jetons* or tokens to pay for calls.

The next morning, I found her waiting for me in the lobby of her rather smart hotel, the Édouard VII on the avenue de l'Opéra. What a friendly and well-spoken girl she was, and so very English she seemed now that I had become a "seasoned" Parisian. Over coffee in the lobby, we worked out what we ought to see in the day and a half remaining before she flew back to London. After only a fortnight in Paris, it tickled me to think that I was about to become a personal city guide.

We went first to see the collection of works of the Impressionist school in the Jeu de Paume gallery in the Tuileries Gardens. It was only a short walk away: down to the rue Danielle-Casanova; then along a brief stretch of the avenue de la Paix into the quiet elegance of the place Vendôme with its Napoleonic column and the shopfronts of some of Paris's greatest jewellers; and then under the arcades of the rue de Castiglione, across the busy thoroughfare of the rue de Rivoli and down the few steps at last into the gardens.

How wonderful it was to have such a pleasant excuse to go back to the gallery so soon. I had been there but a week before and could now show Jennifer some of my favourite pictures: Toulouse-Lautrec's poster of La Goulue as she danced the cancan; Manet's *Joueur de fifre* (which I had always liked); Monet's *Femmes au jardin* (which looked so fresh and clean, so sunlit) and his series of the *Cathédrale de Rouen* painted in different lights and moods and now hung side by side to stunning effect; and Van Gogh's self-portrait with its wavy background. It was entertaining to hear someone else's reactions to the works of art. Seeing on display in the gallery paint-bespattered palettes, long-handled brushes and half-spent tubes of oil colour that had belonged to some of the Impressionists soon had us talking about the creative processes involved in painting in oils and the new ways in which these artists used pigment to capture the effects of light on landscapes, seascapes and on the lineaments of the face.

After a fine meal in a restaurant under the arcades on the rue de Rivoli, we made our way to the pont-Neuf to catch a Vedette boat for a river trip on the Seine. It took a while to find our way down to the landing-stage. Down some steps we went and there at last was the boat, not large but with plenty of windows, moored to a pontoon deck. We joined the motley group of tourists on board and off we set on a smooth ride downriver, taking in all the famous sights from an unusual angle. We sailed as far as the

Eiffel Tower and then turning round sailed upstream as far as Notre-Dame and the île de la Cité, listening to commentaries, in French and English, German and Italian, on the sights on the Right and Left Banks as we slid past.

Back in the opulence of the Édouard VII bar, Jennifer and I had a chat with the bartender and ordered a couple of Dubonnets. At the next table a middle-aged American gentleman wearing smart casuals overheard our conversation in English and proceeded to butt in. A Connecticut man born and bred, he sat himself bolt upright and slightly wiggled his shoulders as he proudly announced that he was working in the world of computers.

"My name is Drew, by the way, and I work for 'Ibby Bibby Machines'!"

Those were still early days in the use of computer technology for business and somehow his nickname for one of the biggest and fastest emerging computer firms in the world, seemed so irreverent and too familiar, and rather belittled his executive status of which he was patently proud.

We went for a stroll along the boulevards towards the café Le Brébant and ended up at what had already become one of my favourite small restaurants in the rue du Faubourg-Montmartre for an early evening meal.

Never a sufferer of dyspepsia, you can imagine my mortification when our delicious meal of steak and chips was cut short by a sudden burning stomach-ache, but thanks to a dose of Fernet Branca supplied on the house by an unperturbed waiter, I was raring to go next morning when I picked up Jennifer at the Édouard VII.

We began our day by going to Montmartre. Walking up the hill we were both disappointed: what we saw, though steeped in history, was squalid, even slatternly. Only its ugliness gave it a redeeming "charm". But when we reached the place du Tertre all our misgivings were forgotten for the real Montmartre was all around us. In a small tree-filled square with cafés on all sides were artists of different types working in the open for all to see their work. We looked at all the paintings and the standard was fairly high. Some, though, we agreed, were either too experimental or rather hackneyed. There was clearly a market for all the work being shown and particularly for silhouettes by a skilled cutter (but not my scissor man in the Tuileries Gardens), who was much in demand.

There was to be more disappointment, this time in looking round the Sacré-Cœur. The panoramic view of Paris was far more appealing than the basilica itself. A magnificent lunch afterwards sitting in the shade of the trees in the middle of the place du Tertre made up for all shortcomings, including our further disillusionment as we went down the hill by another way, past a small vineyard (much to our surprise) and several derelict windmills.

We called by René's office to say farewell. Jennifer's flight home from Orly was that afternoon, and I was booked on a mid-morning boat train the next day. Another Dubonnet at the Édouard VII, this time with a slice of lemon and oddly diluted with Indian tonic, and it was time to take Jennifer to the airport on the Air France bus.

*

As my varsity autumn term began, so too did a yearning to find myself a Parisian job for the following summer. When things had calmed down over the Christmas vacation, I thought there would be nothing to lose in dropping Ronald Buckley a line at the Banque Française du Commerce Extérieur. There might at least be a chance that I might be able to gain experience of working in Paris if Mr Buckley were to go on holiday in September the following year. How would I be able to convince him that I was the man for the job? So, I wrote a simple letter outlining my plans and reminding him of the temporary vacancy I had applied for too late in the September just gone by.

Several weeks later, I received an airmail letter with a Paris postmark with my address below it neatly written with a fountain-pen in turquoise-blue ink. I carefully slit open the envelope, pulled out the letter and unfolding the pale-blue sheet saw that it was written in the same hand with Ronald Buckley's signature at the bottom. Its style, to me at least, suggested many years of training in the offices of the diplomatic service. He apologized for the "dustiness" of his reply to my letter, but given my student background, he would be more than willing to take me on for the duration of his holidays. Quite naturally, there would be a bit of overlap at the beginning when he could explain to me everything I needed to know, and a little bit at the end to ensure a smooth handover on his return. Would I be capable of undertaking this work, I wondered, and in such an unusual setting?

8.
Clive settles in Salies-de-Béarn

In spite of my misgivings, Salies-de-Béarn was in fact a bustling, pretty little town. Some of its older houses boasted rickety first-floor terraces which looked down on narrow streets linking a string of small squares. In the largest of these the weekly market was held. Old houses in the middle of town overlooked the quietly flowing Saleys river. I ought to mention, by the way, that this was a thermal resort famous for the beneficial qualities of its waters. It was then a popular place to take the cure and many still go there today to do just that.

I had plenty of spare time to soak up the atmosphere of the town. Most weekends I was the only one to be staying at the residence. My colleagues went back home whilst their pupils enjoyed forty-eight hours in the bosom of their families in the outlying villages that dotted the Béarn. Left on my own I was never remotely bored.

The Saturday market was always a day of great activity. The townsfolk, their numbers swollen by the inhabitants of neighbouring villages, congregated in the market square. The stall-keepers were rightly proud of their produce, some of which came from their own farms and market gardens. A large multicoloured selection of fruit and vegetables was piled high on their stalls. All this bounty came under rigorous and relentless inspection by ladies of advancing years, some wearing the black weeds of widowhood. They did not think twice about fingering and prodding the fruit and vegetables to see if they were ripe enough, something that reminded me of Soho's Berwick Street market in London, but where the barrow boys would forbid any handling of their goods or else you would be told off in no uncertain terms. For the first time in my life, I saw live rabbits and hens up for sale, all of them cooped up in tiny wicker cages and staring out blankly at the passers-by, unaware of their imminent fate. I found it hard to imagine that the average English cook would be ready to buy a living creature at the market and take it home to slaughter it on the kitchen table!

While the old ladies were busy chatting about family matters as they did, almost incessantly, while doing their food shopping, the old men gathered around café tables on the market square, as they drank their draught beer and berated their political leaders.

Lounging in a capacious wickerwork armchair at the biggest café in town, the Blason, on the nearby place Jeanne d'Albret, I could easily while away an hour with a coffee and that day's regional newspaper, the *Sud Ouest*, as my only companions. It sometimes crossed my mind as I sat there that I had not had a conversation in my own language for months. There cannot then have been any other native English speakers living for miles around to talk to, and it struck me that it must have been just the same for Peter over in Montréjeau. I smiled to think that I had become so immersed in the French way of life that I had even had a dream in which I was actually speaking French.

For clients in the café, the toing and froing of passers-by was an endless source of interest. What a great opportunity for them to keep an eye on what their fellow townsfolk were up to! Those who happened to be there when the coach from Pau halted just opposite were offered another spectacle. And what a great opportunity it was to observe people from all walks of life! There were neatly clad businessmen, countryfolk with laden baskets; there too were the young coming back from the big city.

The café had a large, varied clientele. Marcel, the owner, was a likeable fellow, always ready to spend a couple of minutes chatting with you. Whenever he spotted me out on the terrace, he always came right over with my usual *café au lait*. He could not help but make references to the current British political situation, always prefacing his remarks with the jocular comment:

"So, Monsieur Wilson, how are things? Do you think Britain will one day join us in the Common Market?"

I guess that it was in the nature of his job to know a little something about all of his customers and what they got up to, whether of an innocent or scandalous nature.

I was not the only language assistant at my school, for there was also Marisa from Spain, who ran the Spanish conversation classes. Since neither of our working hours were too onerous, we left school at the same time and often went and sat for half an hour at the Blason for a drink. Most of the time we chatted away in Spanish and that definitely helped my fluency.

We would talk about our respective university lives and studies. Marisa would talk about the customs and traditions at Salamanca, her ancient and distinguished university, and I in return would give a perhaps over-embroidered account of all the wonderful activities on offer in Swinging London. Inevitably our discussions sometimes veered into the domain of politics, and I was hugely relieved when she told me that her family was in no way supportive of Franco's regime.

"I cannot bear even thinking about that man," she exclaimed. "At his hands a member of my family was locked up for a short while because of his political views."

There were some days when customers at the café might observe us boarding the coach to Pau together. That alone was enough to set tongues wagging among certain nosy residents of Salies, who, seeing us so often together, had mistaken the nature of our friendship. In truth, I knew that Marisa was glad to have a male chaperon, Spanish style, as she travelled about. Nevertheless, the rumour still went round that ours was obviously a relationship of a deeply romantic nature, and there were even some who claimed she was my mistress! Nothing could be further from the truth. They would have felt very let down to know that ours was a purely platonic relationship. They were unaware that my romantic yearnings were reserved for another young lady who lived in a far-off city and who was totally unknown to any of them!

As the weeks went by, I became attuned to the pace of life of my adopted town. Believe it or not, I was not missing London life that much. In any case, I had regular news updates from home. There were exchanges of letters or postcards, or when things were more urgent, there were telegrams and international phone calls. For the latter, you had to pop down to the post office in Salies.

When I made my first call from there, I had not the slightest notion of how difficult this task would prove to be. At the desk, the telephone operator told me that making an international call was no easy matter and that you sometimes had to wait a good while before getting through. And believe you me she was right! At long last, after waiting a full quarter of an hour, I heard the operator shout out:

"Call for England; go to booth number two, please."

I did as I was told and went over to the booth. On finishing my conversation, I went back to the counter to pay for my metered call.

That evening at dinner, I told my friends about my first international telephone call and what a to-do it had been. After hearing what I had to say, they began to chuckle.

"Be careful, Clive, we always say that the operator is fully informed about everything. On the face of it, she does seem to know everything that is going on around here! She's a bit of an eavesdropper!"

"Oh I see! I was wondering why she was always butting into my conversation and saying *allô* and *ici Londres . . .*"

All the same, I hoped that she only had a passing acquaintance of my mother tongue, for I was pretty sure she was hanging onto my every word.

On Saturdays and Sundays, there was obviously no provision of the usual delicious meals at the residence, for all the pupils had gone home and Madame Lagourgue certainly deserved her days off after her supreme culinary efforts during the week. So, in order to assuage my hunger pangs, I had to sort things out for myself. That meant that I had to check out what the various cafés and restaurants in town had to offer. But I had already got to know the Auberge du Paradis since sometimes, when we fancied a change of scene on a weekday evening, a bunch of us would go there for dinner. The owner was a most welcoming woman, who served us dishes of the highest quality.

When I was on my own on a Saturday evening, I would still go there before heading for the small picture house in the middle of town. I was a bit of a film buff, and back in London had frequented the Academy Cinema on Oxford Street, where foreign-language films were often screened. I was already acquainted with French cinema and the films of the New Wave directors: *Les Quatre Cents Coups* by François Truffaut; *À bout de souffle* by Jean-Luc Godard. And now I had the opportunity to see the latest offerings of famous directors like these as soon as they were released in France. After I had tipped the usherette, I would sink into my seat for a couple of hours of sheer escapism and enjoyment.

The evening ended with the usual walk up the hill to Mosquéros, the silence occasionally broken by the barking of a vigilant dog. Finally, I arrived, the residence standing shrouded in darkness. Only the whispering of the breeze amongst the leaves in the trees and the sound of my steps on the gravel driveway broke the stillness of the night.

Once in bed, a quietness surrounded me, interrupted every now and again by the sound of creaking rafters. As I lay there, my thoughts began to wander. They kept coming back, not to Marisa, the Spanish girl here in Salies, but to Marianne, the French girl there in Toulouse. Even with my eyes shut, I could see her face. Her presence seemed so near, in spite of all those miles which separated us. I wanted to be with her so much.

But my yearnings were dispelled by other thoughts. Worries about how my future life might turn out rose to the surface, as did worries about what lay in store for me. But these preoccupations always yielded to the overwhelming power of sleep.

9.
John's apprenticeship at a Paris bank

With a screeching of brakes, the long Ligne de Sceaux suburban train pulled into Antony station, seven miles south of Paris. Mr Ronald Buckley and his partner Rolande had invited me to stay the night on the eve of my temporary contract at the Banque Française du Commerce Extérieur.

There could be no mistake; I knew who he must be straightaway. Slim and of medium height, he looked the perfect English gentleman. There he stood on the platform, informally but smartly dressed, wearing a cashmere pullover and sporting a cravat, and accompanied by a brown dachshund on a lead.

"I'm Ronald Buckley from the Bank," he said, shaking my hand, "but do call me Ron!"

At their house on the rue de la Cité Moderne there was Rolande busy making the dinner. She was a kindly and welcoming Basque lady, with a strong personality. Their home was a pebble-dashed bungalow, all spick-and-span, small but furnished in good and unpretentious taste. It perfectly complemented the character of the couple. And, as with so many other houses in the southern suburbs of Paris, theirs was surrounded by flowerbeds with a low fence separating their home from the gravel path beyond.

Here, for the first time in my life, I was experiencing the daily routine of underground train, work and sleep that the Parisians call "Métro, boulot, dodo", but now, as you might say, in reverse order! We set off next day, Ron and I, from Antony station; he was now wearing a suit and I was more modestly attired in jacket and trousers. We alighted at the huge underground railway interchange of Auber, not far from the Opera House.

"We are very near the office now," said Ron, reassuringly, "but first, let's go to the Bank's head office on the boulevard Haussmann. After that, I shall take you over to the translation department; it's in an annex on the boulevard des Capucines."

On reaching ground level, we came out onto the boulevard Haussmann, with the department stores of Printemps and the Galeries Lafayette dominating the other side of this busy thoroughfare. We crossed at the main junction, with the back of the Opera House on our right. At last, we reached the great granite doorway of the bank at number 21.

Even before crossing the threshold, there was Ron greeting people in the street who, I supposed, were his colleagues at the bank. I could not get over the sheer scale of the place. Ron had already given me an idea of what the bank was all about. Shortly after the Second World War, the French government had set up this bank to grant credit facilities as part of its plan to reconstruct French industry and to re-establish France's role on the international financial markets. I never found out how many people worked at the bank, but I soon saw there were what seemed like hundreds of employees.

Could there be anything more fascinating than leaving the business areas open to the public and going behind the counter, perhaps to enter a hidden world of high finance? Already as an amateur actor I had had the experience of waiting in the wings to go on stage, and I was later to witness as a staff member the true goings-on in a great London museum, on the other side of the ropes.

But a few steps away from the majestic sweep of counters where men and women in formal dress were talking respectfully to customers in hushed whispers, we entered a maze of rooms of all shapes and sizes, where hordes of clerks were working surrounded by heaps of paperwork.

"Let's start with Mrs Clément," said Ron.

I followed him down long passages and up and down steps. At the end of this journey that I feared I would never be able to repeat on my own without the help of a compass, we reached the personnel department where Madame Clément, a lady who was probably nearing retirement, greeted me, peering benignly at me through her Perspex-rimmed spectacles.

She had a manila folder ready waiting for me, with my name handwritten in large elegant sepia letters on the outside. The great ledgers of a Dickens novel sprang to mind. I was to enrol in the French social-security system, and an URSSAF, or national insurance number had already been allocated to me.

Next, I had to meet the director to whom Ron was answerable for the translation department.

"Monsieur Colignon, I am delighted to introduce you to Monsieur Adamson, who is standing in for me while I am away on holiday," said Ron, after we had stepped into the director's spacious office. In the dim light cast by the lampshade, I made out the form of a middle-aged man. He rose from his chair behind his vast desk on which there were only a few scattered files and a calendar, and came towards us, his hand outstretched.

"Ah, Monsieur Adamson, welcome to the BFCE, I hope you will enjoy being with us."

"Thank you," I answered somewhat tremulously.

"Now, let's deal with practical matters," Ron said to me, taking me to the bank's own social services department. "You'll need some restaurant vouchers."

As it turned out, given the modest level of my employment, I was entitled to buy one-franc vouchers, and for a few more centimes I could treat myself to bread and a small bottle of wine to go with my meal.

Finally, the time had come to go over to the translation department. We left the bank through the staff entrance in the rue de la Chaussée d'Antin, turned left, walked past the Paramount cinema on the corner and after a few yards went through the big doors of no. 5, boulevard des Capucines. After having gone up the wide staircase with its elegant metal banister, we went through the white-painted double doors leading into the bank's annex. Across the threshold there was a landing with a fitted grey carpet. A man in a lumberjack's shirt was standing in front of shelving stuffed with thick buff folders each tied shut with white ribbons and each of them marked "épuré". That must be something to do with processed transactions, I thought. He had one folder, its ribbon untied, in his hand. We greeted him, opened another white panelled door, and went into the translation department.

It was made up of a small string of rooms painted white, all of which had tall double windows looking out onto a courtyard. Out of the corner of my eye I glimpsed a couple of reassuringly familiar posters pinned to the wall. Published by the English Tourist Board, they depicted photographs of Big Ben and of a Beefeater on guard at the Tower of London. I could detect a slight whiff of stale cigarette smoke in the air.

Maryse, Mr Buckley's secretary, broke off from the busy clatter of her typing, stood up and came over to say hello. She was tall, and very Italian both in complexion and warmth of character.

Ron was beaming as he said in English: "This is Maryse. She looks after me and helps me with English translations. She will be a great help to you."

"Welcome, John," she replied, also in English, but with a pretty accent.

"Let me introduce you to Madame Flec," Ron said, turning towards a slim and smartly dressed small dark-haired lady who was coming over to us. "She will be responsible for all the administration in my absence. If there is a problem of any sort, she will deal with it. Now let me introduce you to Laurence who looks after German and Dutch translations," he went on. "And this is Madame Cléret, who works on Spanish and Portuguese texts."

I had now shaken hands with everybody in the team of that time. Apart from Madame Flec, this team was to make up the core of the department for a number of years.

Before heading to the canteen to sample the dishes of the BFCE, Ron suggested I should spend a little time looking at the kind of work undertaken by his department. I could never have imagined the wide range of tasks involved. Letters from banks all around the world passed through this department to be translated into French. Most of them were in English, of which a number, true to American style, always commenced with the greeting "Gentlemen", others in a rather more abstruse style came from banks in the United Kingdom, and there were others written in a form of English that varied according to where in the world the letter came from. For the most part, this correspondence was about setting up huge letters of credit to fund all manner of projects in France and abroad. Sometimes, there were contracts drawn up in English to be put into French. But the heaviest and never-ending workload was translating into French what were known as "renseignements", or credit status reports on individuals supplied by other banks. An ability to fulfil financial obligations seemed the crucial attribute. The translations were typed up on rolls of light-green gummed paper and then affixed to index cards.

"Now let's go for lunch," said Ron. "Maryse, will you hold the fort while we are at the canteen?"

And off we went for the eleven fifteen sitting.

When we came back, Maryse went off for a later sitting to have lunch with her mother, who worked in another department at the bank. This she did most days, and I always enjoyed watching the short preparatory ritual before she set off. Her capacious black handbag was at the ready; a quick look in her hand-mirror was followed by a deft adjustment to her mascara and lipstick; then out came her Chanel spray. The tiniest of squirts of this precious fragrance onto her neck and wrists and she was ready to go out, with what seemed to be the height of Parisian chic. All this ritual was quite new to me and yet seemed so natural. I had never worked in an office before nor ever witnessed a young French woman making herself look even more sophisticated. Looking up from my papers, I was rather impressed by this little spectacle.

As my first day at the office drew to a close, Maryse asked me: "I hope you didn't find the day too long, did you?" Far from it, I had been intrigued by the novelty of it all and could not wait to witness more of her Parisian sophistication as well as learn more about the work that was being done by the translation team.

My first taste of life as a French civil servant at the BFCE lasted only a month or so. Quite often after my copious lunch in the canteen, I would wander down the boulevard to the Madeleine church and sit on the steep steps outside in the early autumn sunshine browsing the pink pages of the office copy of the *Financial Times*. Whenever I looked up, I could see all the way down the rue Royale to the tapering red granite of the Luxor obelisk in the Concorde square. I felt like a banking executive, but in truth was no more than a 20-year-old student needing to mug up on the world of finance and its vocabulary in two languages – and fast. Sometimes I would idly step down to the square below the Madeleine and watch the card-sharper at his orange box outside Durand's music shop as his billfold of banknotes grew fatter by the minute.

I was able to repeat my experiences of "high finance" the following summer during Mr Buckley's annual leave, and the summer after that as well. And then my employment at the bank resumed for two further occasions when Mr Buckley was off sick.

Each time the work was pretty much in the same mould. There was one important development in the sense that in the course of my stays, I was gradually able to handle the translation from French to English with greater ease, and then, with Maryse's help, I began to do the translations of important contracts from English into French. I reached a stage where I could dictate my translations in either language to Maryse. She was a true mistress of stenography, and, with Mr Buckley's backing, had just followed a course in how to adapt French shorthand to take down English. Soon she could cope with English dictation too, from Mr Buckley or me, scarcely batting an eyelid at the new challenge.

I had no idea of the importance of these contracts that dealt with enormous sums of money. It was a matter of understanding clearly and then putting across the meaning of the text. In a relatively short span of time, I had in effect followed a training course that had given me a depth of knowledge of the world of trade and its vocabulary in several languages. I mastered the art, and an art it truly was, of writing letters and commercial documents in English and French and besides which, I managed to acquire a smattering of other languages in this financial setting. Coin by coin it was a piggy-bank of knowledge that I was accumulating; amounting to something which has served me well ever since.

One day, in the middle of a morning on perhaps my third or fourth stint at the bank, a lady from the staff office brought in a small, dapper man in his early middle age. He was clutching a capacious leather brief case with big flap and buckle on the side.

"This is Monsieur P –," said the lady.

It turned out that it had been agreed that Monsieur P – should be relegated for a while to the Service des Traductions. A spare desk had been allotted him, but no work assignment. He sat down, deftly adjusting his pin-striped trousers as he did so, pulled out a copy of *Le Figaro* from his leather bag and spent the whole day leafing through the newspaper. For the weeks he was with us in the department, he came in every day and sat reading his newspaper, pausing occasionally to chat to Maryse.

I never did work out why he did not have a proper job of work to do beyond warming his seat but was earning a salary from the bank.

Yet none of us begrudged him his idleness – indeed I believe we all felt rather sorry for him.

He was charming and always impeccably turned out in his pin-stripes just like any other senior business executive.

What anomaly was it that lay hidden away in the cryptic world of *fonctionnaires* which allowed him this odd existence? Yes, working for the BFCE, a state-run bank, this secondment to our office reminded me that we were all civil servants. Was he somehow shielded from being forced to leave the bank by some obscure clause of French employment law?

Every so often, throughout each working day, a young office boy brought us our correspondence. This was usually stapled inside flimsy brightly coloured folders known as *chemises*. Each "shirt" clothed a translation to be done. Some executives would thoughtfully send useful supporting documents attached to the translation. I liked this sharing of background information that eased our task, and as I separated the documents, I would smile to myself at the metaphor the French used for a paper clip. *Trombone* so aptly described the humble office device, both in its shape and its sliding motion.

Once in a while, a dark-red folder would arrive from the bank's chairman and managing director, Monsieur Jacques Chaine. When one of these was delivered, you always had to open it there and then and deal with it immediately. Each time there was a letter inside to someone of great importance that was to be translated into English. Each time the letter was sent along with a few special blank sheets of the chairman's own special headed notepaper for Maryse to type out the letter in English. If by chance she made a mistake, or *faute de frappe* as typing errors were called, there was headed paper enough to make a pristine copy. Painting over the mistaken letter in white would never have done. These letters were less of a financial and rather more of a diplomatic nature. For my part, I strove to find the best turns of phrase that I could muster.

How deeply shocked was I to learn some years later that Monsieur Chaine had been assassinated by a political activist one morning outside the door of the nearby Crédit Lyonnais bank on the boulevard des Italiens, where he had not long been chairman.

A happier story about the BFCE, also after my departure, was the discovery made the following year when work was being undertaken to restore the bank's newly acquired Hôtel Moreau, a splendid eighteenth-century town house on the rue de la Chaussée d'Antin. In the courtyard a mysterious ridge was opened up to reveal the heads of statues. François Giscard d'Estaing, cousin of the former president of France, was a director of the bank at the time and something of an amateur archaeologist. He was able to establish that the heads had come from Notre-Dame.

The story went that in the early 1790s revolutionaries had mistaken the Gothic sculptures of the kings of Judaea from the galerie des Rois on the west front of the cathedral for the kings of France. The statues were taken down and dumped in fragments outside the cathedral, with their heads removed, together with statuary torn from one of the church's doorways.

André Malraux, who had served as minister of cultural affairs in de Gaulle's first cabinet of the Fifth Republic, had known the story of the statues but had nursed the theory that they had then been buried somewhere in the mud of the Seine and would one day be dredged up. Sadly, he did not live to learn that instead what had happened was that the heads and some other fragments had been bought as rubble at the time by the owner of the town house, who, seeing what was in the rubble, had painstakingly and respectfully buried the relics. The heads and other fragments are now in the musée de Cluny.

10.
Sad news for Clive from London

Most afternoons I was the first among my colleagues to get back home to Mosquéros, for the others had many more teaching hours than I did. Mind you, I could easily have devoted more of my free time to doing the supplementary work that Mr Shrimpton, my Spanish lecturer in London, regularly sent me! He was naturally hoping that I was not completely neglecting my Spanish during my French escapade. This work was hurriedly finished, I must confess, in order to meet the deadlines he had set me, and popped into one of the yellow postboxes of the PTT just in the nick of time.

At that stage of the afternoon, the kitchen of the boarding-house drew me like a magnet. The agreeable aromas wafting out of the open door and windows set me thinking about the delicious food that was to come. There I would find the ever-solicitous Madame Lagourgue bent over her kitchen tasks. She was always more than ready to spend a few minutes chatting with me. She was genuinely interested in my welfare and wanted to be sure that I was not too homesick. On each visit, I loved the way that she spoilt me: "Eat some of this, Monsieur 'Cleeve'! Have a drop of red wine. Ça remonte le moral. That'll lift your spirits," she used to say, pressing me to have a quick snack with the drink, without of course spoiling my dinner.

One autumn afternoon, after a good natter with her, I went over to my house, and there on the hall table was a letter for me.

It was in Malcolm's handwriting. Good friend from college in London though he was, I was surprised that he had written to me. Tearing open the envelope, I read the first few sentences and then stood there frozen to the spot.

> I have some dreadful news to tell you. Emile has died. He fell ill suddenly. He had lung cancer and it was all over in three months. The cancer raged through him like wildfire. There was nothing that could be done to save him. . . .

My mind went blank, and then threw up an image of Emile at the Kingston swimming baths. We had met on the first day of training of the water-polo team and had become good friends. He was a tall, well-built man; in his green eyes there was always that good-natured gleam. Together we had endured those long hours of training, which were so exhausting. We had played in many matches, all of which were fiercely contested. He never lacked courage when the team was on the attack. And when the match was over, it was always the same routine. The whole team would head for the pub. We would joke and tease each other; conversation was always lively, fuelled by pints of bitter.

Grief overcame me. How could it be that he had died at such a young age? He was the same age as me: twenty-one. I struggled to come to terms with this absurd loss and raged against fate that had cut him down in his prime. There would be no more joyous Saturday nights at discotheques or at parties, always in each other's company. Still clutching the letter, I felt so alone and so far from London and the support of my friends there. The realization that I would never see him again made it all the harder to bear.

11.
Cinéma vérité: on location in Paris

On my last long stay at the Paris hostel, I heard that French film-makers occasionally took on extras. The idea of taking part, albeit in a very small way, in a film shot in France seemed at the time to be a marvellous idea and, you never could tell, might just be the first step along the path to stardom!

One morning I caught the Métro to Boulogne-Billancourt and went into the huge cinema studios, which had rather taken over part of this district on the outskirts of Paris. The security guards pointed me in the direction of the production office. With nothing to lose I knocked on the door. A woman's voice replied: "Come in!"

I did as she said, pushed gently on the door and found myself face to face with a somewhat stern-looking middle-aged lady.

"I have come to see if there might happen to be a small role for me in a film," I began quite boldly.

"And why should I consider you for a role?"

I can no longer recall quite what I said in answer to her, but I stammered out something along the lines of: "I've been told that now and again you need extras; I have done a bit of acting and I am really keen on cinema!"

"Yes, it is true that we do take on people as extras but only for short-term work and at very short notice. Would you be available?"

"Yes; most definitely!"

"Right, let me take your details. Your name and address. Do you have a photo of yourself? Can we contact you easily by phone?"

"Well, I'm staying at the UCJG hostel, where you would be able to leave a message, and there is a switchboard number."

"That's far from ideal. Let's leave things like that for now. We'll call you if we need you."

Thereupon, I stood up, said goodbye to her and left, thinking to myself that that would be the end of the story and of my future career as a film star.

But much to my surprise, the story did not end there. A friend of a friend working in the cinema world had heard that I was looking for a small part and must have mentioned it to the production manageress, for a few days later there was a telephone message for me.

I rushed over to the nearest telephone booth at the hostel and inserted my token in the slot.

"Could you put me through to the production manageress, please."

"Speaking."

"It's John Adamson here, you rang me."

"Yes, Monsieur Adamson, that is right. I am inviting you to come to the studios to talk about a film for which we will be needing extras."

I set up an appointment and soon found myself back at Boulogne-Billancourt.

"We're in the process of shooting a film by Pierre Granier-Deferre, starring Jeanne Moreau, Sydne Rome and Alain Delon, for which we need extras," she said.

I was already dreaming of being among these stars of the big screen, quite at my ease as the cameras whirred.

"It's a thriller," she went on, "and we need a whole bunch of men dressed in CRS police uniform."

A tingle shot down my spine. At the back of my mind, I still vaguely remembered the ruthless behaviour of that police brigade in the riots of May 1968, and I shuddered a bit at the thought of having to wear such a uniform with all the sinister implications that came with it.

"Uh, yes, all right," I answered.

"You will have to get yourself a short haircut and go to the address that I shall give you to pick up a uniform in your size."

I cannot quite recall where exactly I had to go to. But I do remember that it was a vast room crammed with clothes of all descriptions for hire to stage and film actors. The place was rather stuffy, and the whiff of second-hand clothes caught my nostrils. The female assistant was very efficient and from among the endless rows of uniforms of the Compagnies républicaines de sécurité hanging there, she found me one of the right size, and also handed me a truncheon and shield.

On my first day of shooting, there I was once again at Boulogne-Billancourt, but now dressed up as a CRS officer just like so many other extras. Together we formed the backdrop on set to a scene that was unfolding in a mocked-up backstreet. After a long wait, Alain Delon came out of his caravan. I was really taken aback to find myself in close proximity to such a well-known cinema actor. He had film-star looks all right, with his open, handsomely chiselled face, his impeccably groomed dark hair and his dazzling greeny-blue eyes, but I was not expecting him to be so short. I marvelled at the contrast between the cinematographic stature of this leading man and his real height.

What they were doing was shooting two short scenes from the film. For the first, Delon and Claude Rich got into a black Citroën DS and drove down the narrow street at high speed. A stunt man, or *cascadeur* as they say in French film studios, suddenly leapt off the pavement and onto the bonnet of the car as it went past.

The producer was not happy with the take and they had to do two more. At the third attempt, the stunt man hurt himself, falling and banging his head on the kerb. When I saw that happen, I was very glad that I was merely an ordinary extra.

And then, Delon and his colleague got into another DS which had been specially sliced in two. Like that the cameraman could film the interior of the car, set up a movie scene in front of the car and simulate very heavy rain hammering against the windscreen in the great tradition of those black-and-white thrillers from the 1940s and 1950s.

The second day's filming took place away on location. The whole team of extras disguised as CRS men met up at Boulogne-Billancourt and boarded the same type of coach which was used to transport real CRS. We crossed Paris, heading for Napoleon's tomb just behind the Invalides palace. We were all having fun on the way, chatting, laughing and speaking in loud voices. I had a conversation with two young men who were about to open a small art gallery opposite the Trinité church. But deep down, I felt rather ashamed to be going around like that with truncheon and shield. Passers-by took us for real CRS and made no effort to hide their contempt. I felt like opening the window and telling them: "But we are only extras in a film!"

On the immense esplanade in front of the tomb, we lined up in serried ranks and slowly advanced as one threatening mass of overlapping shields and raised truncheons . . .

After the shoot the production manageress came up to me and said: "If you want to continue having a role in this film, you had better get yourself a shorter haircut."

12.
Clive back in the vineyard

My recent work at the vineyard of Château Beauregard seemed to have greatly interested some of my colleagues at school. I soon understood the reason for this, for some of them had inherited a few acres of land on which they themselves grew vines.

Bearing in mind all the knowledge that he thought I must have gained from my job as grape-picker at Château Beauregard, Marcel Saule, one of my colleagues at the school, invited me to come and give a hand with the harvesting at his father-in-law's vineyard on the outskirts of Salies.

When I arrived at the vineyard early on the Saturday morning, there was already much hustle and bustle as the grape-pickers started to gather. Friends and family were there, chatting and joking, all of them with wicker baskets slung over their shoulders and secateurs in hand ready to set to work. Some of the older women were also far from idle; they were busying themselves with an equally important task of getting the lunch ready. Some were peeling vegetables whilst others were stuffing garlic-filled chunks of bread into plump chickens.

At nine o'clock the picking began. All of us willing volunteers, we worked at a steady pace. Many of the pickers were old hands at the job, some of them airing their considered opinions on the quality of this year's grapes whilst fondly recalling the best vintages of former years. Their conversations were to me highly illuminating, for at this harvest I was very much the one with the least experience.

Time passed by and after five hours not a single bunch of grapes was left on the vines. We heard a woman's voice summoning us to take our places at a large cloth-covered trestle table standing in the shade of the house. No need for a second bidding as we had all caught the whiff of roast chicken and garlic. Once seated round the table, we were soon tucking in and slaking our thirst with wine from this very vineyard! And how delicious it was! Our feast was rounded off with a vast cheese board and a mouth-watering apple tart.

Time was still on the march and dusk stole in, but we hardly noticed. Thc rows of vines, now stripped of their fruit, had begun to blend into the shadows. It was time to go. Hugs and handshakes, and Marcel's father-in-law's heartfelt thanks hung in the warm early autumn evening air.

Several weeks passed by and I had given little further thought to my second go as a grape-picker. I was sitting in the staff room reading the *Sud Ouest* newspaper, when Marcel came up to me and said, "My father-in-law would like you to come and taste the new wine. He thought Friday evening would be suitable. Are you free then?"

I assured him I most certainly was, convinced that this would be yet another instructive experience.

We reached his house on the outskirts of Salies at seven o'clock. When he opened the door, I saw that he was still dressed in his blue overalls. Seeing him standing there, it made me think that bright blue denims like his were more pleasing to the eye than the dreary dark blue overalls worn by English factory workers. He wore his like a badge of pride to show that he was of peasant stock.

After having greeted us, he led us into an outhouse, switched on the light and there, at the far end, was a row of oak barrels lying on their sides. Before them on a small round table stood three glasses.

"Now Monsieur 'Cleeve', this is the moment of truth," he said with a twinkle in his eye.

He went over to one of the barrels, opened the tap and filled the glasses one by one. We each took a glass and began to drink. Rolling the wine round my mouth it tasted soft and fruity, and it seemed innocent enough. This only encouraged me to have another glass – and another. My conversation became quite animated.

"I bet you haven't got any wine like that in England, have you?" he asked tauntingly.

I kept my nose in my glass. The wine kept flowing, and at first my French seemed to be flowing too. I found myself putting together sentences of a complexity of which I did not know I was capable. And yet, this drink did not seem that strong, but then, all of a sudden, I had difficulty stringing together my words in French. My thoughts in English were also beginning to become befuddled.

It was just as well that Marcel lived a stone's throw from my lodgings. At the end of this lively evening, he saw me safely to my front door. Luckily for me, I had a work timetable that did not require me to be present for the four hours' teaching which took place on Saturday mornings!

13.
New waves for John

Washing my face that morning, the mirror was not lying. The fact was indisputable. My hair was a bit too long and one lock of hair was down to my eyes. I needed a haircut.

A short stroll down the rue de Trévise from the hostel there was a small, traditional men's hairdressers, probably with only two barbers, if I remember rightly, who always seemed to be busy whatever time I went by.

By then, I was already used to some aspects of Parisian life like going to the baker's, the post office, and of course to restaurants, but as I pushed open the door of the hairdresser's I had a slight feeling of trepidation.

"Do have a seat, we'll soon be with you," said a man with very short white hair, who, I presumed, was the owner.

Soon it was my turn to sit in the barber's chair and lean my head forward over the washbasin and feel the repeated streams of warm water running through my hair, followed straight afterwards by a vigorous rubbing dry.

Some strokes of the comb were then administered, and I was asked:

"Which side would you like your parting?"

I guessed what he meant but the word he used in French, "la raie", went on conjuring up in my mind a large wing of fish served in a black-butter sauce, for that was also the word for skate!

"Uh, on the left side."

In a trice the haircut was over, and the barber was busy drying my hair.

"You have got very nice-coloured hair," he said.

In a funny way I felt flattered but at the same time I felt abashed, for I did not want to draw attention to myself, and at that very moment, I would almost have preferred to have had a head of mousy hair.

*

A year or so later, once I was settled into my flat in the Marais, my sense of living the full Parisian life was reinforced. For quite some time I had noticed the large hairdressing salon on the boulevard de la Madeleine, going by the name of Coiffures Joffo. Through an immense shop window you could glimpse a whole team of professionals, both men and women, as they tended to the hairstyles of their clients. It was a bustling scene only to be augmented by the reflections in huge wall mirrors. I really wanted to have the experience of having my hair cut at Joffo's. Wasn't it another facet of the elegant way of life of the capital city?

I went in.

A beautiful dark-haired young lady took charge of me. First came the washing. From a flask she poured some amber-coloured shampoo into her hand and rubbed it into a white lather on my hair. As she rinsed it out thoroughly with warm water over the washbasin the sweet smell of chamomile filled the dank air. All of this was repeated. Then came the rubbing and drying of my hair with towels.

"Monsieur Jacques will be cutting your hair," she said.

And yes, it was Monsieur Jacques who did my hair, also asking me beforehand on which side I would like my parting.

When it was done, I heard the swart-haired girl say as she scrutinized my neat haircut: "But your hair is very fine. It's rather flat-looking. What you need is a mini-wave."

"Er, can you tell me what that is?" I enquired rather perplexed.

"To make your hair look thicker, we'll give you a light perm."

Calling to mind the high helmets that ladies wore at that time when they wanted a perm, I dithered somewhat, and I was anxious about the costs involved.

She must have guessed what I was thinking.

"It's done quite quickly with tiny curlers. And it only costs a few francs more."

I am not sure if the thickness of my hair was of greater concern to me than the amount of time that the girl would spend on it. I had not banked on a lengthy hairdo. Nevertheless, I gave my assent, and for the only time in my life a few tiny curlers were put into my hair and my hair wound round them.

When it was all done, the girl took out the curlers, combed my hair and showed me the fruits of her work in the mirror. Yes, it was true: my hair was now wavier and yes, it looked a little bit thicker. That was all. Or was it?

Later that morning, I was waiting to cross the busy junction by Old England, the outfitters' shop where Ron Buckley bought his suits, when whom should I bump into but an old university friend, Penny Rutherfurd, on a flying visit to Paris. Her own locks, long, brown and flowing, looked the same as ever.

"I spotted you in the crowd right away!" she began, reassuringly, with a smile. I heaved a sigh of relief.

Every time I came to Paris, while that salon was still running, I had my hair stylishly cut at Joffo's, and was always recognized and warmly greeted by Monsieur Jacques – but I did without the "mini-perm".

14.
Clive on a Mobylette to the Basque Country

Michel, a young *moniteur* at the school, owned one of those lightweight motorcycles they used to make in France in huge numbers and called the Mobylette. Now, Michel was a generous-spirited fellow and often urged me to go for a ride on it whenever I wished. By doing that, he would say, I would get to other neighbouring towns as well as nearby places of interest. To begin with, so I would get used to it, I would drive his Mobylette through Salies, going round and round the town. Its throaty sound echoed down the alleyways, drawing the attention of passers-by.

When the local policeman saw that it was me riding by, he did not wave me down as perhaps he should have done, but simply shrugged his shoulders, took off his kepi and scratched his shaven head. There could be no doubt that he was in despair at this "breach of the peace", but what could he do since there was an *Anglais* in the saddle!

My town of Salies was not very far from the Spanish border. Spurred on by the countless conversations I had had with Marisa, I had a growing feeling that it was high time that I went back to Spain and had a look at that country once more. And I was particularly intrigued that even closer, virtually on my doorstep, was yet another culture – and even another people. This was, of course, the Basque Country, which paid little heed to the political and geographical frontiers between France and Spain. What is more, it was a region where they spoke a mysterious language that was neither Latinate nor Germanic.

Saint-Palais was the nearest Basque town to Salies. Now that I had learnt to ride the Mobylette, I thought that I was ready to travel the not inconsiderable distance separating the two towns. I set off in high spirits on Michel's Mobylette amid the loud raucous din from its exhaust shattering the stillness of the Béarn countryside. Only the crowing of a cockerel outdid the clamour I was making.

As a trip it had its enjoyable moments. The empty country road went up and down the small hills and gave me the opportunity to gather considerable speed when going downhill. With the wind in my hair and the sun on my face, I lost all sense of danger. And so it was, bent over the handlebars, intoxicated by the speed of my descent, I had failed to notice a hairpin bend rushing towards me. But it was too late: I realized to my horror that at the speed I was travelling I could not negotiate the bend. There was absolutely nothing I could do. The Mobylette careered off the road and headed into a cluster of oak trees. After what seemed like an eternity, I found myself rejoining the road. It was nothing short of miraculous that I had been able to survive taking this involuntary shortcut without smashing into a tree and, would you believe it, without falling off.

Deeply shaken, I set off again but continued on my way to Saint-Palais at a considerably slower pace. Still thankful that I had come out of this unscathed, I parked the Mobylette in the town centre and walked over to the market square.

A sea of black berets swirled about me, and my ears were assailed with a language of which I understood not a word. Still in a state of shock, all this just added to my confusion, and the beret, to my mind, something so quintessentially French, had taken on a new meaning when proudly worn by Basque men.

I had the impression of being in a different world: there, in Saint-Palais, even the French were foreigners.

Knocked sideways by my misadventure on the road and by the strangeness of this country, I had built up such a thirst that the first thing was to make a beeline for one of the cafés on the market square. As I picked my way through the horde of beret-wearing Basques to reach the bar, I could tell right away that I was an object of curiosity. The conversation at the bar quickly ebbed away and I felt that all eyes were focused on me.

"A, a ham s, s sandwich," I stammered in French, "and a, a small beer."

"Certainly, sir," replied the barman without more ado, "that'll be with you in two minutes."

He blurted out something to a fellow barman that must have been my order in Basque.

After an hour's recuperation, I continued my journey, still heading south towards the mountains. For sure, this was beautiful countryside. Verdant, imposing hills rose up all around me, with herds of white sheep seemingly glued to the hillsides high above me. Climbing still, and stopping momentarily, I looked upwards and was astonished to see vultures and buzzards, buoyed by thermal currents, wheeling effortlessly overhead against the bright sky. I rode through charming villages: their houses Alpine in appearance; their ochre-coloured half-timbering criss-crossing their facades. This country was such a thrilling discovery that I felt as though I could have journeyed on to the very highest peaks of the Pyrenees.

But it was growing late in the day and reluctantly I turned around to take the road back home at last. I reached Salies as night was falling.

15.
John and the elusive film world

Emboldened by my participation in the film *La Race des seigneurs*, or *Creezy* as it was known in the English version, I grew more ambitious. I had heard that Luis Buñuel, the veteran Spanish director, at that time living in exile in France, was about to make another film in Paris, a sequel to *The Discreet Charm of the Bourgeoisie*, which starred Stéphane Audran, one of my favourite French actresses. I rushed over to the Billancourt studios to see if I could be an extra once more. This time, however, it was a different administrator, hidden away in an office right at the end of a long corridor. At his beckoning, I went into his office.

"I am sorry, sir, but Monsieur Buñuel is no longer taking on anyone else for his new film. Everything is now under way."

And so, *The Phantom of Liberty* was released without me! I kicked myself for having just missed out on it. I would have so liked to have worked with that great filmmaker.

Nevertheless, my cinematographic career did not end there, but took an unexpected turn.

Michael, a London-based English film entrepreneur, and his wife, Yvonne, were busy promoting a film treatment that told the story of a gaucho in the Argentine pampas. He already held an option on the screenplay and was adamant that the role of the lead actor should be played by Alain Delon. Michael did not know Delon at all, and what is more he could hardly speak a word of French.

So, I was given the job of making contact with Delon with a view to negotiating a contract. It was easy enough to find his agent in Paris, easy enough, surprisingly, to arrange a meeting with him in his fine, vast office on the quai des Grands-Augustins with its commanding view of the Seine.

In actual fact, on this occasion and on many others, the ability to speak French provided me with a weapon that enabled me to be bolder and aim higher than I might have done in my native tongue. On opening my mouth to speak in a foreign language, I was hiding parts of my make-up which would automatically be revealed if I were speaking English. I exploited that for all it was worth.

"Well, sir," said the agent, "we are seriously interested in your colleagues' proposal. I shall speak to Monsieur Delon about it, and it could be that I shall be inviting your colleagues, and yourself as interpreter – congratulations by the way on the high standard of your French – to Monsieur Delon's residence at Aix-en-Provence to talk further."

Only a few days later I had a letter from the agent. And so, Michael, Yvonne and I travelled down to Aix.

As night was falling our taxi rolled up outside the Hôtel du Roy René, where we were looked after majestically by the liveried porter. He had just finished showing a fellow guest how to fold a jacket without creasing it: by turning the garment inside out and tucking one shoulder into the other. Something I had never seen done before, and so effective. Once we had checked in, we ventured forth, walking down the scent-filled streets of the town, a little of the day's heat still lingering in the twilight. The great summer festival in Aix was in full swing, and the atmosphere was intoxicating. At last we reached the place des Quatre-Dauphins where a Mozart opera was being performed in the open air. It was a struggle to make our way through the jostling crowd, but on one corner of the square we found the door we were looking for and rang Alain Delon's bell. Before we knew it, a very pretty girl opened the door and bade us come in. On reaching the first floor, she led us into a fine panelled room, its walls sumptuously hung with tapestries and paintings and asked us to sit down at a stately, carved wooden table.

As soon as the agent I knew from Paris arrived, we started eating a delicious light meal, at the same time talking about films and eventually about the proposition.

"I am sorry that Monsieur Delon is unable to be with us this evening, but he would like to thank you very much for being given the opportunity to star in the film. He wishes to express through me his interest in playing the role of the gaucho. He would of course like to have a closer look at the screenplay and then talk terms."

On that note, the meal and the meeting drew to a close and we went off full of hope.

I caught an Air Inter flight to Paris very early the next morning and turned up, with a copy of *Le Méridional* under my arm, at the usual time at my much more ordinary and less attractive office of the translation department ready to carry on with my linguistic work surrounded by commercial documents.

As for Alain Delon, he stated his terms, but sadly the proposal never got off the ground.

*

A love of film brought me two more interwoven cinematographic moments, each with a Parisian dimension. Only a few months after Joseph Losey's film *The Go-Between*, with screenplay by Harold Pinter, had won the Palme d'or at Cannes, I saw it in Paris. Watching the turn-of-the-century tragic tale unfold sitting in a small Latin Quarter cinema was seeing an imagined English past in a foreign country. I watched the film with English eyes and ears and an inborn affinity with the rolling Norfolk landscape even though I had yet to go there.

For all that, I was aware that the audience around me was witnessing a story and a setting that would have seemed alien. The haunting music by the French composer Michel Legrand added to my mounting sense of foreboding. Did the French audience feel the same way about the film score? Or was there something in the music that was quintessentially French and therefore familiar to counterbalance the Englishness of it all?

Not long afterwards, Losey and his English wife sojourned for a while in the Latin Quarter. René Saint-Maur delighted in telling me how he had been approached one evening by Joseph Losey in a small restaurant on the rue du Dragon for a part in the film he was planning of Proust's *À la recherche du temps perdu* with screenplay by Harold Pinter. Sadly, that movie never came to fruition, but Alain Delon starred with Jeremy Irons in *Swann in Love*, a screenplay by Peter Brook of Proust's novel released more than a decade later.

Perhaps Losey's approach had been half in jest, but it did show that this filmmaker had a good casting eye. Who did he have in mind for René, I wonder? Could it have been the duc de Guermantes who struck such a magnificent monocled figure at the Opéra in Pinter's screenplay?

My Losey/Pinter connection did not end there, however, for many years later I published under my own imprint *Norfolk Summer: Making The Go-Between*, as part of the celebrations for the fortieth anniversary of the royal premiere of the film in Norwich. After the screening of the newly restored film at a Norwich cinema, it was fun chatting to Dominic Guard at the celebratory dinner held at the Maids Head. As a 14-year-old he had played the part of Leo and was still instantly recognizable.

As for René François-Saint-Maur – to give him his full family name – he became both friend and mentor over the early years of my career. He was always there in the background whenever I was in Paris: avuncular, sympathetic, for ever forthcoming with sound advice and ideas, only a telephone call away; and what proved so particularly helpful was how he gently urged me to be adventurous on my career path and not to be afraid to ask.

But René kept his cards very closely to his chest and so it was only many years later that I found out a little bit more about him. There was certainly an inkling of Major Marmaduke Thompson about him. That caricature figure, the brainchild of Daninos, first published in the columns of *Le Figaro*, epitomized a certain type of Englishman abroad, well, at any rate, an old-fashioned ex-army Englishman living abroad, as imagined by one Frenchman.

René was rather proud of creating an illusion of a certain Englishness. You had only to listen to his clipped manner when he spoke in English; or witness his aristocratic bearing; and smile at his delight in having once been taken for an English major in Trafalgar Square. He was not so happy when he found that his so utterly French daughter Anne had begun to speak English with an American accent, having wed an American and moved to the States.

Yet the René whom I knew was not a military man but a man of the world, and of the commercial world at that. When I first met him, he had already written one book (on the cardinal points of marketing) and followed it ten years later with a book on statistics in salesmanship. And after all, that did make sense, for when we first met, he was working for Richard Nelkène, the man credited with coming up with the idea of advertising at the point of sale.

He made little of his privileged upbringing. While his elder sister Hélène followed in the footsteps of their father and became mayor of the community of La Boissière-du-Doré in the Loire-Atlantique, where their family seat stood, René had been drawn early on to life in the metropolis. Nevertheless, he brought with him a great gift for words no doubt inherited from his father, who had trained as a lawyer and who, for a score of years, had served as senator for what was then the Loire-Inférieure region.

When I first met René, he was living as a *résident permanent* in a room at the Hôtel Édouard VII, but by the time I came back to Paris the following year to begin my first stint at the bank, he had rented a flat on the avenue du Roule in Neuilly-sur-Seine on the western rim of Paris. It was only a short walk from there to what must have been his "cantine", Les Gourmets des Ternes.

There in this charming bistro in the seventeenth arrondissement, Francis, its bespectacled, welcoming owner, would find us seats, me on one of the long red upholstered benches along the wall and René facing me in one of those curved-back bent-wood bistro chairs, while waiters would serve us delicious hearty fare. René would order a chilled bottle of Côtes du Ventoux and we would tuck in, chatting away merrily on every topic under the sun. Neighbouring diners would eavesdrop on our conversations, intrigued by René's remarks, and be entertained, as I was, by his witty turns of phrase. Sadly, all of that is almost beyond recall, but one lunchtime at the tail end of one meal, René engaged in banter with the waiter as he ordered the cheese course for us both.

"What is the *fromage du jour*?" he asked.

"Cantal," came the reply.

That was a hard cheese from the Auvergne, not unlike good Cheddar. I nodded approvingly.

"Then, let's have *deux Cantaux*," said René, playing on the plural ending for "cheval" as in Deux Chevaux.

It was in those early days of computer technology, and I remember standing at the entrance to the Ternes Métro station after one of our joyous meals at the Gourmet des Ternes, discussing the reduction of language – and thus of all things in their description – to the binary system of notation, a switching between only two states of being.

There was also the occasional meal at his ground-floor flat with one or two other guests. Over a glass of Tomatin we found ourselves trying to work out what the difference was between *hibou* and *chouette*, and finding none, wondering how it had come about that there were two words for an owl in French.

René proudly unhooked a smallish painting off the wall to show me. It was a portrait of Hélène painted by my father when he, my mother and brother had gone to La Boissière-du-Doré one summer after visiting me in Paris. It was an intriguing likeness of a rather stern lady, but of one who, like René, had patently a good sense of humour and always something interesting to say. But she, too, like her brother, hid her talents under a bushel. One day, years later, browsing among my late mother's French books we found a copy of *Un Cœur méconnu*. This book was a translation Hélène had done in the 1950s of Florence Montgomery's *Misunderstood*, a Victorian novel made into a film by Jerry Schatzberg in the 1980s. She had dedicated it to my mother, in grateful memory of my grandmother, she wrote, who had taught her English.

What was to become a farewell gift, sent to me in Cambridge by René, was a Livre de Poche edition of Julien Green's *Suite anglaise*, a miscellany of essays about great but eccentric English writers. "I would be surprised if you did not find the book interesting," he wrote on *Sélection du Reader's Digest* notepaper. He shared my fascination for Green, a Paris-born American who had chosen to write in a language that was not his mother tongue.

Later that year my mother received a letter from his sister Hélène to say that René had died in the night of an *infarctus*. He was still only in his sixties.

16.
Béarnaise sauce

When I first arrived in France I knew precious little about French cooking, to be honest, but it soon became clear that my three housemates really did. They were keen to take on the not-too-daunting task of instructing me in this domain. René, more than the others, seemed to have an almost encyclopaedic knowledge of the restaurants offering the tastiest food in the Béarn. Time after time you could hear his voice ring out in the early evening: "We're going out for a meal!" That had all of us scrambling towards his car, a Deux Chevaux, parked as always just outside. I never had the faintest idea where we were going, but it was with total confidence that I left it to my "culinary masters" to make the choice of eatery. Markedly less was my level of confidence when it concerned the breakneck speed the car was driven.

Such finesse in the preparation of the food set before me was inconceivable before coming to France. On every restaurant outing my friends waited to see how I would react to each course. It was often local fare of which they were justifiably proud. And so, for the first time, I tasted hearty country pâté, snails, duck's thighs, omelette with red peppers and both goat's and ewe's cheese. It was a similar story when they introduced me to wines, urging me to sample wines from a variety of vineyards. Among the white wines they gave top marks to a Jurançon produced in the Béarn, and from among the reds they often chose a full-bodied Corbières from the Languedoc.

At first, I struggled to get used to the odd aniseed taste of pastis, their favourite *apéritif* and a much-loved drink in the south-west of France. René would present me with a tall glass containing a small splash of amber liquid. Next, from a squarish jug he would pour in a measure of water and I would watch fascinated as it was transformed into a long milky-coloured drink. It was only thanks to his perseverance that I was eventually converted, for in the end I did come to like it, much to his delight.

Sometimes after the meal there was an impromptu singalong. This was a tradition that I had never come across before, but I joined in the chorus as best I could. I can still recall some of the racy verses from "En revenant du Piémont", but the words of a pretty song in Basque which I sang parrot-fashion have sadly faded from my memory.

As we returned from one of these merry autumn evenings – it was a journey like so many others with swathes of mist shrouding the unlit road home, and some of us dozing off – we were suddenly jolted into wakefulness as the car braked sharply. In the beam of the car's headlights we saw a Mobylette lying on its side in the middle of the road. But there was no sign of the motorcyclist. We all came to the same conclusion: there must be somebody lying injured nearby. We halted and got out of the car. Then began a thorough search along the verges, all of us stumbling about when we were plunged into darkness behind the car's headlights. At last, we came upon a body, stretched out inert on the grass below a stone wall. "This could have been me," I thought with a jolt, as I recalled my close shave on my Mobylette journey to Saint-Palais. Everybody looked worried.

"He's dead!" uttered a shaky voice.

As I looked more closely at the elderly man, I was able to reassure the others that on the contrary he was still breathing. I spotted a gaping wound on his forehead encircled with dried blood. I saw that he was now stirring a little without groaning.

There we were in the middle of nowhere and far from the nearest telephone and none of us had had any training in first aid. We felt we had no choice but to take him to the nearest village to find help, and so together we lifted him up gently and put him on the back seat next to me.

Meanwhile, it fell to me to try and find out who he was and where he lived. He had difficulty replying to my questions, no doubt because of his accident, but also of the effects of alcohol that I could smell on his breath.

We carried on to the next village, where we spotted a man out walking his dog. René drew up near him and wound down the window.

"Excuse me, Monsieur, we have just picked up a man who has been in a road accident. He's there on the back seat. You wouldn't happen to know him, would you?" shouted René.

The old walker came over to the car and leant inside.

"Heavens above, it's Henri! Just look at the poor fellow. I hope he is not too badly hurt!"

As luck would have it, Henri did not live far away, but on a farm just outside the village. Armed with directions, we reached the farm within a couple of minutes and carefully took our injured passenger out of the car. I held him up, locking his arm around my shoulder as we made our way across a muddy yard, waking up a gaggle of geese, who rushed towards us, hissing threateningly. We knocked loudly on the farmhouse door. After a short while, a woman in her dressing-gown cautiously pulled the door slightly ajar, looked us up and down without saying a word and then exclaimed:

"Ah! That husband of mine! This is not the first time that this has happened. Come on in, gentlemen."

We stepped across the threshold.

"Now, what will you have to drink?" she said.

It was all of one o'clock in the morning!

17.
John, the gourmet banker

The canteen at the bank was a saloon on the rue de la Chaussée d'Antin near the bank's staff entrance set up as a plain and simple restaurant. Executives sat six to a hexagonal table and against the convivial din of animated conversation tucked in just like great food buffs, all this for the paltry price of a restaurant voucher.

In the thick of it all Monsieur Ali, a charming, efficient and moustachioed Moroccan always wearing a white waiter's jacket, dashed about trying to serve everybody at table. An impossible task, in truth, but among the waiters and waitresses he was king and the most in demand.

At unbelievable speed, he arrived at each table and reeled off the dishes of the day: veal stew, turkey, chitterling sausage, chicken in wine. And for anyone who did not want to indulge in these dishes, there was always what was known as the *régime*, a diet of standard fare that was always the same: a fried steak with French beans.

On every table there was a plentiful supply of various yoghurts, some petit-suisse cheese, some bottled water, and for those who had purchased a wine voucher they could select a 17.5 centilitre bottle of a decent red that was brought to the table.

The banking executives were lacking in patience.

"Monsieur Ali, can I order now?"

"Monsieur Ali, what's on the menu today?"

And Monsieur Ali, striding round the tables, balancing a

laden tray on one hand, replied:

"I'm on my way!"

On my first day, Mr Buckley introduced me to Monsieur Ali.

"Be sure to look after John while I am on holiday. He is standing in for me."

"Of course I will! With great pleasure."

"Monsieur Ali!" somebody shouted.

"J'arrive!"

I had no cause to complain, for from the very first time I met him and throughout each of my short-term contracts with the bank, he was amazing in the way he looked after my culinary needs. He quickly noticed that I had a hearty appetite and when he saw my empty plate after having devoured the dish of the day offered me whenever I wanted it the standard regimen of steak and French beans at no extra charge!

After my first meal in the canteen, Mr Buckley invited me to a nearby bar for a "café-Calva", a celebratory coffee with a thimbleful of Calvados on the side. There, leaning on the zinc counter, an impeccably turned-out man with an open face already had his coffee cup to his lips.

"Ah, Monsieur Disy, let me introduce you to Monsieur Adamson, who is going to stand in for me in the department while I'm on holiday. If you need any English translation, don't hesitate to get in touch with him."

"Delighted to meet you, Monsieur Adamson, delighted."

We shook hands.

When our coffees were served, conversation switched to the internal politics of the bank. I was out of my depth, unable really to understand quite what they were talking about. Whenever Mr Buckley alluded to the smallest problem in the department, Monsieur Disy came out mechanically with the same laconic reply: "C'est du mauvais classement, Buckley, mauvais classement. You can put it down to bad filing."

*

What had begun as temporary accommodation for my job-finding trip to Paris became a more permanent base over several visits to the city to work at the bank. The UCJG was ideally situated being only a twenty-minute walk away from the bank. Far from luxurious, it was cheap, cosmopolitan and companionable. The friendships I made there had an influence in some way or other on the course of my life. Even when on my second stint at the bank Maryse let me stay for a peppercorn rent in the small apartment in Pantin she had bought as an investment near the Porte de la Villette, or the time when I put up at a small hotel in the second arrondissement, the UCJG was still a great place to go to meet my friends. Not for nothing was it known as a *foyer des jeunes*.

To me as a lover of fine cooking, there are two culinary incidents that stick in my mind from my days at the hostel. At the time of my first stay there, Les Halles were still the prime marketplace for vegetables, meat and fish, all of them housed under the roofs of Baltard's renowned iron-pillared pavilions. Nothing could be easier than crossing over the main boulevard late at night and going down the rue Montmartre as far as the Saint-Eustache church. There, amongst the porters, the trollies, the stacks of cabbage boxes, amongst the sellers, the shouting and the smells, it was at the Pied du Cochon restaurant on the rue Coquillière, opposite the round stone building of what had once been the corn exchange, that York-Gothart (or York for short) and I ate our onion soup. I think it must have been the first meal I had had with him outside the hostel. I would of course see him there every morning in the small downstairs breakfast-room, where he earned himself a few extra francs by preparing the *petit déjeuner* for all the guests. He would nonchalantly toss his long flaxen hair to one side as he prepared bowls of milky coffee and *tartines beurrées*, that morning's freshly baked baguettes sliced lengthways and buttered, while he bantered with everybody in an endearing German accent, an ironic smile lighting up his face.

Between spoonsful of hot soup, I caught a glimpse, a little further along the street on the corner with the rue Jean-Jacques Rousseau, of a shop sign in big yellow capital letters that read E. DEHILLERIN. The heavily shuttered frontage of the shop gave no clue as to the Aladdin's cave of kitchen equipment inside. It was only walking past the shop one day when it was open that I glimpsed the great copper pots and pans gleaming in the window, a spectacle that set me thinking how such a wonderful *batterie de cuisine* like this evoked that French passion for fine cooking accomplished with fine utensils. Only many years later did I pluck up the courage to venture into the shop and discover for myself the wealth of glorious tools for the kitchen of the professional chef, and only then, when my budget allowed, did I begin slowly to build up my own collection of steel-lined copper ware.

By then, I am sorry to say, Les Halles was no longer a vegetable and meat market and so a magical juxtaposition of raw produce and fine cooking had been irretrievably broken. As York and I sipped our hot onion soup with its *croûtons* and grated Gruyère cheese we had absolutely no idea about the planned changes that so soon were literally to tear out the heart of culinary Paris.

Along the rue du Faubourg-Montmartre, only a few steps away from the UCJG, there were restaurants, cafés and bars galore, to suit all purses; French cooking cheek-by-jowl with north African.

There, on the other side of the street was a dimly lit courtyard at the far end of which stood what I believe to be one of the most typical restaurants of old Paris. I had often passed by it and had vaguely noticed its white neon sign, but one day Henri, a stocky ex-Foreign Legion soldier and fellow guest at the hostel, suggested we should go there and have a bite to eat.

Pushing open the restaurant door, we entered a quite different world: a huge hall of mirrors, of chandeliers and skylights, and of countless tables where guests were tucking in. We were inside the Chartier restaurant, where neither the atmosphere nor the décor could hardly have changed since the early twentieth century. Across one of the wall-paintings, almost worthy of François Boucher, there flew a small bi-plane frozen in time. Over much of the eating area daylight came flooding in through the vast skylights.

A waiter took us over to a large table with chequered tablecloth overlaid with a simple white paper covering, around which there must already have been at least ten people busily eating and chatting. He left us with a long bill of fare in thick closely-knit handwriting stencilled in blue. If I remember rightly, I chose the raw vegetable salad or *crudités* and a steak. You had to write what you wanted to eat and drink on the paper lay-over; then the waiter committed to memory what you had written and shouted out the order to the staff at the cash desk and in the kitchen. The food was hearty and tasty without being anything outstanding; and it was fairly cheap. The restaurant had grown out of being a *bouillon* serving simple soups and stews to local workers and artisans at the turn of the twentieth century to one serving hungry office workers and tourists at modest prices. When the time came to pay, the waiter came over to tot it all up, putting a price to each line of the order we had written on the paper table covering. This turned the transaction into an act of mutual trust. But keeping a watchful eye over all the proceedings, a stout lady with pearl necklace sat majestically behind a great ornate till.

18.
Clive rolls up his sleeves in the provinces

After all the excitement of the grape harvest in the Pomerol and my arrival at Salies, you could be forgiven for thinking that my stay in France was just one long holiday. Far from it; I had clearly defined teaching duties at the school. I would need to take my work seriously even though my workload was only twelve hours' teaching a week.

The thought of taking charge of a classroom of pupils did not make me feel overly nervous, for this appointment was not the first one I had undertaken in an educational establishment.

When I was eighteen, having passed all my exams in French, Spanish and History at Colchester Royal Grammar School, I was qualified to apply for entry to a British university. But, being of a rebellious spirit, I had other plans. Much more appealing was the idea of moving to swinging sixties London. Anyway, I had made up my mind to find myself a job there, earn a bit of money and have the freedom to do whatever I wanted.

I took up the offer of a clerical job in an insurance company in the City, in the heart of that famous Square Mile of London. I must admit that I was not expecting this work to be particularly appealing, but at least I would earn enough each month to enable me to live in a modest way in the capital.

Given my knowledge of foreign languages, I was set to work in the international business section of the company. My career in insurance was short-lived, for I found the work I was given to be exceedingly boring, and I loathed the stifling ambience of being in an office. When ten months were up, I had had enough of it and so, without more ado, handed in my notice without quite knowing what I would do next. Not for a moment did I wish to give up my London lifestyle, yet somehow or other I had to pay my rent.

A fortnight after I had left the company, I was sitting on the Tube idly reading job vacancies in the evening paper when, by sheer chance, I spotted that a job had become available in a boys' school which I knew to be only five minutes away from my lodgings. The school was seeking a classroom assistant. On the spur of the moment, I made up my mind to apply for it.

I was called to the school to meet the headmaster, who offered me the job there and then. And that is how I took my first steps along the professional path that would shape my life. As it transpired, I worked a whole year there under the tutelage of a grey-haired man of medium height called Mr Cass. He seemed to me to be rather elderly and at first glance you would say that he did not have any distinguishing features to speak of. But beware of jumping to conclusions too quickly. The fellow was a maestro in the classroom; he could anticipate every devious trick of the ebullient East End boys in his care. He readily shared his wisdom and management skills with me, callow young man that I was, who hung onto his every word. Little by little, he asked me to give extra tuition in English, arithmetic and history to groups of four or five pupils at a time. Thanks to his exemplary mentorship my confidence went from strength to strength.

With this teaching experience behind me, I was not that nervous about standing in front of a classroom full of young French pupils when I fetched up in Salies a few years later. In the London school, the behaviour of some of my pupils had sometimes been quite challenging. This stemmed in some instances from their difficult home backgrounds. On the other hand, it was easy to see that with these small-town pupils in rural France it would be unlikely that I would encounter the same sort of problems that teachers sometimes faced in London. What is more, my fellow English-language teachers at the school in Salies, who were native French speakers, had been most forthcoming in volunteering ideas and teaching tips which would help me in the classroom. They were most enthusiastic about having a native English speaker among them to supplement their own teaching programme.

As teaching aids, I had brought with me a stock of various linguistic games for the youngest pupils, and for the older ones English-language newspapers and magazines to discuss current affairs, which I hoped would arouse their curiosity. At the school I had noticed that the teachers of English followed a curriculum in the classroom that was very clearly drawn up. In France, I was told, teachers were to follow a study programme organized on a national scale. This meant that aims and objectives needed to be achieved within a prescribed timetable which would ensure pupils up and down the land proceeded in their studies at the same pace. I soon got into the swing of things, however, and the weeks rolled by without my even noticing.

As I went about my work, I made a point of observing how the native French teachers brought out the best in their pupils. René, who taught history, had an innate ability to connect with them and always had time to help those in need of advice and support. It came as no surprise to me to learn years later that he had risen to the rank of headmaster. His skills evidently went beyond classroom teaching.

A sense of firm discipline pervaded not just the classroom but everywhere else in the school. The pupils after all were mostly weekly boarders and a team of *surveillants* or discipline monitors kept a watchful eye on them outside the classroom as well as in the boarding-house out of school hours.

I came to know one of the monitors quite well. Maurice was a shortish man in his early fifties, neatly turned out and sporting a well-trimmed moustache. But I soon learnt that he had been born and had lived most of his life in Algeria. I found out too that he was one of the 800,000 or so French nationals who had had to be evacuated and sent to the French mainland in 1962, when the Algerian War of Independence came to an end. Little wonder that his forced departure from the land of his birth was a deeply bitter experience for him. To have tried to stay on and given armed resistance, he told me, would only have led to a massacre. And yet he now found himself something of a misfit in French society, still with an undiminished longing for his homeland and the life he had lived there.

I was now beginning to understand why René made frequent mention of his older brother's Algerian experiences, and in one of our lively discussions over dinner he told me the belittling term used by some of the French populace to describe these evacuees: "les pieds-noirs".

Back in the classroom, we language assistants in French state schools were nevertheless given considerable leeway as to topics for discussion with our pupils. The main thing, as I saw it, was of course to fire their enthusiasm and encourage them to participate fully. To my satisfaction, my pupils set to with quite some fervour. What is more, their classroom behaviour was always pretty good and so discipline never became an issue. They certainly seemed tolerant of my teaching efforts as I went about instilling the fundamentals of English in them and they readily mimicked what was to their ears the odd sounds of the language. Furthermore, when it came to discussing things which especially caught their imagination, such as pop music or sport, they clamoured to speak English, but all of them at once.

You could hardly call a dozen hours of teaching a week very taxing and, moreover, I had a whole day off in the working week when I was free to do whatever I liked.

Surprisingly enough, in such a staunchly republican nation like France, the comings and goings of the British Royal Family always intrigued them. In fact, they were a bit disappointed when I had to admit in all honesty that Queen Elizabeth was not among my circle of close friends and so I was not in a position to tell them anything about the Royal Family's forthcoming social engagements.

19.
John and the newly-weds

Back in the City of Light, early in February, I put up at the hostel in the rue de Trévise. Nothing had changed: the echo of people shouting in the street reverberating among the tall buildings; the jostling of cars as they parked bumper to bumper; and that characteristic rumbling sound that Paris taxi engines made. And there too was the swishing of a broom as a street-sweeper swirled water along the line of the kerb, carefully guiding it around the wheels of the parked cars. He had begun his task some yards away with a turn of a wrench to open a valve hidden under a lid in the kerb. And now the water gushing out was made to flow in one direction, a rolled-up scrap of sodden carpet serving as a dam.

Once inside the hostel there was still the same slightly disorganized welcome, with the same bunch of long-term inmates in amongst the coming and going of passing travellers.

I soon bumped into Georges, my friend from Toulouse, in the hallway.

"John, did you know that I am getting married? Do you want to come to the wedding?"

"Oh, what a lovely surprise!" I answered. "But who are you marrying and when?"

"An Italian girl. She's called Sandra and she comes from Florence. The wedding is next Saturday at the town hall in the ninth district."

While I had been away from France much of the previous

year, Georges must have met this young woman at the hostel.

"Yes, I did meet her here," he told me in an offhand sort of way. "She came to the hostel towards the end of the summer because she had spent all her money and was awaiting a bank transfer from her father in Italy."

What a stroke of luck that brought these two people together and what courage for them to embark on married life so soon.

"You'll meet her at the end of the week," he went on. "After the ceremony, we're going to celebrate our wedding at the restaurant on the main boulevard. I hope you will be able to come to the feast too."

One evening towards the end of the week, Sandra came to the hostel. I saw straightaway why Georges had been so taken by her. And there she was, a beautiful, fair-skinned woman, with an open smiling face and dark-brown eyes, sitting in the small bar at the back of the lobby. She was soon laughing and joking with everybody, the strength of her character shining through despite her having no more than a mere smattering of French. Whenever she did not understand what had been said, she shouted out "C'ha detto?" and whenever she could not find the right word in French, she asked, "Come si dice?" Georges, on the other hand, did not speak a single word of Italian, but whenever Sandra was at a loss for the right French expression, he resorted to speaking Catalan, the language of his parents, to come to her rescue.

I was very happy for Georges, but I could not help but see that there was a cultural gap to be bridged between them. I felt sure that they would make a go of things yet foresaw a huge challenge ahead for them that would be fascinating.

It was Saturday morning. The February greyness of Paris was at its most dismal. The zinc sheeting on the roofs merged with the metallic grey of the sky. The tall buildings of the ninth, clad in the grime of ages, loomed out of the winter shadows. I do not remember much about the town hall of that district, other than that it was a modest, eighteenth-century building, not in the slightest way pretentious. I sat down in the official chamber with Henri, York, Reinhardt and Roberto from the hostel. There were not that many guests, but I did hear one group speaking in Italian. I concluded that this must have been the contingent surrounding Sandra's parents; and there was also a Catalan-speaking group gathered around Georges's parents.

The civil ceremony was over in a matter of minutes. The young couple came in, sat down before the mayor, made their marriage vows to each other, stood up and went out. Nothing could have been simpler.

There was no official photographer. Without my realizing it at the time, my humble black-and-white photographs taken outside the town hall were the only ones to capture this event. In one of these photographs, you can see Metella, Sandra's mother, wearing a heavy coat with fur collar, looking very much the Tuscan lady. In contrast, the young bride's father, who was Venetian, exuded a very relaxed and worldly charm. By their side stood Ilaria, one of Sandra's friends from university, also wearing a fur coat, though hers was black and heavy. With her typically Mediterranean bearing, her comely face framed by luxuriant black locks, this young lady could not have looked more Italian.

We made our way slowly to the boulevard restaurant, where a large room had been set aside for the wedding feast. I met Georges's parents. His mother was small and slightly built, with short black hair, and spoke French quite passably, whereas his father was a handsome middle-aged man who spoke in a creole of French and Catalan. Georges's parents had fled Franco's régime and had settled in France shortly after the Second World War. His father was an engineer and had had the good fortune to find himself a job in the aircraft industry in Toulouse.

Little remains in my memory of what we ate and drank. What I do recall is the happy and joyful ambience that each and every table shared with the newly-weds. It was then that a deep friendship was forged not only between husband and wife but at the same time between Sandra, Ilaria and me, one that has lasted to this day.

Only many years later did I learn more about the engagement of Georges and Sandra. To some degree they owe their marriage to Ilaria's astuteness. Visiting Ilaria in Canterbury not long after that first short stay in Paris during which she had met Georges, Sandra had recounted to her how this meeting with a young Frenchman at the hostel had completely bowled her over.

As Ilaria said to me: "Do you know, John, all she knew about Georges was his Christian name, and that he came from Toulouse. And that was everything! And over what remained of the summer holidays Sandra had no idea how she would be able to meet him again. 'If you really want to see this boy again,' I had explained to her, 'you'll need to find out his surname and after that his parents' address in Toulouse, and then try and get in contact that way. Let me help you.'"

Ilaria had shut herself in a Canterbury telephone booth and rung the UCJG in Paris to see if anybody knew Georges's surname. Then, with the help of international directory enquiries, she had been able to find the only family going by the name of Casas in the whole of Toulouse. Rather than making a telephone call, Sandra, almost on the spur of the moment, caught a train from Canterbury to Dover, the ferry to Calais and trudged across France by train all the way to Toulouse.

It was there, in the Toulouse suburbs, that she had found the little house belonging to Georges's parents, had knocked on the door and asked if Georges was in. Happily, the answer, after this odyssey, was in the affirmative.

After they got married, there followed long walks through Paris, which from today's standpoint turned into a series of cosy outings to the Closerie des Lilas. At least I can remember all of us there in the bar, sitting with our aching feet around a couple of tables with small brass plaques, one recalling "Guillaume Apollinaire" and another, "Paul Fort". The former was quite familiar to me, but the latter meant nothing. I did not know that he was also a poet and belonged to a literary clique which met at the Closerie. Nevertheless, I could sense an atmosphere steeped in the history of fascinating individuals for whom this was their very own café.

I loved the multicoloured garlands that adorned the floor tiles and the impressive display of bottles behind the bar. On the counter there was a small advertisement to say that they served Bass beer here. And that brought to mind the famous painting by Édouard Manet called *Bar des Folies-Bergère*, in which beneath the reflection of the man ordering his drink, a bottle of Bass beer on the marble counter is clearly recognizable from its triangular label.

But we only ever ordered hot chocolate: what a delight it was all the same to drink this smooth beverage made with melted chocolate and whipped milk!

20.
Clive tries his hand at rough shooting

When I was a boy my family and I occasionally went to spend a few days at my grandfather's house over in neighbouring Hertfordshire. In his garden there was a small shed in which I had noticed an air rifle and next to it a round tin containing lead pellets. My grandfather had spotted my fascination with this gun and one day decided that at eleven years old I was ready for him to give me a shooting lesson. Our targets were empty tin cans that he put on the ground some fifteen yards in front of us. I took aim, I fired, I heard the clinking sound as the pellet pierced the side of the tin. Needless to say, from that moment on, I was hooked on mastering the skill of shooting.

For my fifteenth birthday, my father very generously bought me a .22 air rifle. He had been aware of the extent of my interest in shooting and perhaps he had concluded that I was now responsible enough to follow my sport without the need for supervision.

Nevertheless, I had to be careful when shooting because ours was a small town-garden and I dreaded causing injury to the neighbours.

The following year, the problem went away when we moved to a house that my father had had built in the country about six miles south of town. The house stood in a plot of about a third of an acre, where I enjoyed total liberty in following my sport without any risk of causing harm to others. My grandfather came over to stay with us from time to time and very often we would have a shooting competition. Even at seventy-five years of age, he was by far the best shot of the three of us.

I should add that my grandfather had also spent some time in France, but his spell on the other side of the Channel some fifty years earlier had been much rougher than mine and had afforded him the cold, wet, muddy and perilous comfort of the trenches. He had landed in France in April 1917 as an infantryman in the Honourable Artillery Company, just in time to take part in the battle of Arras; his ability to shoot so well was honed since he was allotted the task of being the first Lewis gunner for his section.

The field and woods around our house were heaving with all sorts of game. There were pheasants, partridges, rabbits, hares, and of course pigeons galore. On certain autumn and winter days shooting parties would appear circling the small wood across the field from our house and you could hear bursts of gunfire.

But theirs was a somewhat socially exclusive form of shooting, the reserve of landed folk and City bankers. They were kitted out in a rather odd, even comical way. They wore Oxford brogues, long, knee-length stockings in green or beige wool, tweed golfing plus fours and a jacket and flat cap also in tweed. Of course, I could hardly mix with people of that sort! Be that as it may, very often, some of those same pheasants, and the rabbits and pigeons too, used, out of curiosity, to come on to our land, and obviously my father and I did not have a moment's hesitation in taking advantage of this bounty!

The first time that I got my hands on a shotgun, however, was during my stay in France. One autumn weekend, Peter had invited me to come over to Montréjeau, where he was teaching, and savour the rustic delights of the Haute-Garonne. One of the teachers at his school had ostensibly lined up a country walk for us. He came bright and early to Peter's lodgings to pick us up.

As we drove off, Roger wasted no time in telling us the true purpose of our outing.

"I am a great lover of rough shooting, you know," he told us. "And today I'm inviting you to come along and join in."

All of a sudden, our planned country walk took on a new dimension. This was not at all what we had been expecting. I did not know if Peter had ever shot a gun in his life, and as for me, I only knew how to shoot an air rifle.

"Obviously," Roger went on, "you haven't got guns of your own, but don't worry about that, I've brought along a couple of extra guns for you, along with a good supply of ammunition."

Once I had got over this startling twist to events, I could not wait to widen my knowledge of firearms.

A quarter of an hour later, Roger, our hunter, parked his car at the gateway to a ploughed field and told us that he had shooting rights on the surrounding farmland.

He took the guns out of the boot and handed one to both of us. He explained how to load them. With our jacket pockets stuffed full of cartridges, we set off in single file following the line of a hedge. Our attire was not at all designed for fancy English shooting parties: wellington boots; blue jeans; pullovers and everyday sports jackets.

We trudged across fields and skirted small woods. With a heavy flapping of wings, a pigeon flew off from a branch ten yards away from me. I took aim, followed its flight path and fired. What a disappointment! The bird flew on as if nothing had happened. Mastering the art of firing a shotgun was clearly harder than it looked. The kickback of the butt against my shoulder took me by surprise and I thought that by the end of the day's shooting my shoulder would be blue with bruises.

As it turned out, Peter was no more of a shot than me. He tried to pick off several pigeons in flight but enjoyed no success. By the end of the morning only our seasoned hunter had been able to bag some game: three pigeons, one rabbit and an unexpected quarry . . .

Earlier in the day there had been an incident that had really shocked us. At that time, our host was walking a little ahead of us. We saw him raise his gun and fire at a bird in full flight. We watched the bird stall suddenly and drop in a long curve to the ground.

He picked it up and came strutting towards us. Roger was proudly holding his tiny trophy aloft: it was a thrush. Was he planning on eating that small bird, we could not help wondering?

We kept our feelings to ourselves, however, but deep down both of us were stunned, even disgusted, for in England you never shoot this much-loved songbird, which is strictly protected under the law.

"Thrushes make delicious pâté!" he declared.

21.
John moves house

Every evening a young man of Chinese origin would settle himself down as night porter in the little office at the entrance to the youth hostel to keep an eye on the comings and goings. When I came back in the evening, having eaten out or having been to the cinema, he was always there, welcoming, smiling – and very often playing the classical guitar.

Playing this instrument interested me very much, for a few years before, I had built my own guitar and had learnt to play a little classical music on it. I told him of our shared interest.

"Why not have a go on mine, if you like," he said one evening, when he noticed how interested I was. "My name is Max, by the way. What's yours?"

And that was how the guitar sessions began. It could only be guitar solos, alas, for I had deliberately left my guitar back in England. I had thought it would have been too risky travelling around with it. At any rate, I could borrow Max's and from his stack of sheet music sight-read studies by Fernando Sor.

Max seemed to be leading a fascinating life. Having arrived from the island of Réunion, he had settled in Paris, and to earn a crust was doing several jobs: dock-side steward for Bateaux-Mouches, the Seine's leading cruise-boat company; night porter at the hostel; and what's more he did painting and decorating for a friend and had just completed a training course in bath-room tiling.

In his spare time, he was reading *Quand la Chine s'éveillera . . . le monde tremblera* [When China Wakes, the World will Tremble], the newly published bestselling book by Alain Peyrefitte, who had been the French minister for repatriates in 1962 at the time of the Algerian crisis. It intrigued me that a young man of Chinese origin should be interested in what might happen in mainland China. In those post-Cultural Revolution days, the book title – wrongly attributed to Napoleon – seemed an unlikely prophecy.

I was full of admiration at the range of his activities, without fully realising all the hard work that this entailed, though I think that I must have made more of his work in doing up flats than perhaps I should have done. Undoubtedly it combined practical work with a means of earning some money and supposedly provided him with a steady income. But in my soul it stirred romantic notions of work, of using my hands to make things and of making a living from doing so.

Looking ahead, how was I going to be able to arrange my life better and at the same time have a permanent place to live? And how was I to maintain a sound cash flow?

"That friend of mine who does up flats really came up with a brilliant idea," Max told me. "You know what, he started off here in the big city at this very hostel, stubborn Auvergne lad that he is. His room was up on the top floor. He seemed to be working pretty much night and day, and with the money he saved he went to the auctions and bought himself a maid's room at the top of an old block of flats. Then, in his spare time, he did up the room: he put in a new washbasin and lavatory, updated the electrics and replastered the walls. Then he left the hostel and moved into his newly refurbished room. Now that he had somewhere to live without having to fork out money for rent, he saved up enough dosh to purchase another room somewhere else in the city and did that up too. And so, little by little, he bought rooms here and there across Paris and did them all up. He took me on to give a hand. And then he started renting them out."

My jaw dropped; I could not get over the simplicity of his idea.

"And is he still doing it?"

"You bet he is. Things are getting better and better. He has recently been able to buy a few small flats in the Marais district. Still following the same pattern of restoring them and then renting them out. He has now set himself up in a flat in a beautiful old building in which we restored his own flat and several others besides."

I was very much drawn to the idea of living in the Marais. It was a charming and centrally located quarter which was just beginning to be sought after. I loved the way that it was still a bustling district of craftsmen and skilled manual workers. I had spotted a violin-maker's workshop next door to a mattress-maker's, and in the rue de Sévigné there was still a *bougnat*, a workaday café that besides selling beverages sold coal for home delivery. It brought to mind the *prime de charbon* or coal allowance added to my payslips at the bank, even though I did not ever work there during the winter months.

"Max. I'd like to rent a small flat. Do you think he might have something available in the Marais?"

"You can but ask him. I'll give you his details."

He took a small sheet of paper and jotted down the address: 16 rue Sainte-Anastase in the third arrondissement.

"His name is Olivier, and he lives on the top floor."

22.
Clive and Marianne

Besides my work and getting used to life in Salies there was something else that I was longing to follow up. Marianne. I was missing her so much.

It was in late October that I resolved to make a telephone call to her and dialled the number she had given to me. After a few minutes' conversation, it became clear that we were still drawn towards each other and so we agreed to meet again, this time not at a château but at Toulouse-Matabiau railway station.

Glancing through the compartment window, as the train hurtled towards my destination, I only half-noticed that the countryside was already taking on the subdued shades of autumn, for uppermost in my thoughts was Marianne. Every now and again shadows of doubt stole across my mind. My hope was that our friendship would carry on as before. I wondered if I would be able to chat with her in the same easy way as I had done in our first meetings at the grape harvest.

As soon as I saw her all these doubts vanished. There was Marianne standing under the station clock. I knew she had spotted me in amongst the crowds alighting from the train when I saw her waving in my direction. The way she was smiling at me was totally beguiling. As she walked towards me, I thought she looked even more gorgeous than I remembered her being. Her fair hair drawn back into a chignon, she looked so stylish in her cream blouse and brown mini-skirt.

We hugged, we kissed, and our conversation rolled along in a jumble of French and English, without the slightest lull or awkwardness.

"Let's have a quick glass of rosé to toast your visit," she said, linking arms and leading me into the station bar.

When we had drained our glasses, she said, "And now I am going to show you round what the locals call the 'pink city'."

And so began the first of many visits. That autumn Toulouse belonged to us. Arm in arm, we strolled along the streets and through the squares beneath the gentle warmth of the mellowing sun. Free spirits, we lingered long, sitting at bars. Forgotten in the intensity of our conversations, our coffees went cold.

Marianne loved taking me to art galleries, where she aired her wide knowledge of modern art. As for me, I really loved browsing with her through the antique and bric-à-brac shops in the oldest part of the city. Never mind the fact that the artefacts we saw there were far beyond anything either of us could afford.

Sitting in her presence I was utterly bewitched by her beauty, by her graceful gestures, by the way she tossed her head, her blond hair then falling back into place. I could never tire of being in her company. Whenever she spoke to me in English, I found her accent captivating and I hung on her every word. Whenever I spoke with her in French, she was always forgiving about any slips I made. We talked about her university studies; and when she talked politics, I could detect a real commitment for social justice in her eyes.

"You British are so lucky to have a socialist government in power: free health care; money being poured into social housing. I just wish Pompidou would take a closer look across the Channel," said Marianne.

At dinner time we unfailingly ended up at our favourite restaurant Au Père Louis in the rue des Tourneurs. There we would enjoy sampling dishes of the region, perhaps a *confit de canard* or a hearty *cassoulet toulousain* with its pork sausages, white beans and goose fat, filling and refilling our glasses from a carafe of Corbières wine.

We would leave the cosy warmth of the restaurant and take a short stroll along the banks of the Garonne in the cool autumn air, watching the mists hovering over its waters. This great river bisected Aquitaine, and on its way to the Atlantic, rolled through Marianne's home city of Bordeaux.

We led the life of night owls as we then headed towards the student quarter and to a small dimly lit nightclub. We started dancing rock and roll, holding hands and energetically spinning each other around. And as the night wore on and the notes of the saxophone grew longer, it was the turn of the slow numbers. Entwined in each other's arms, we were lost to time as I held her tight, overcome by the fragrance and warmth of her skin.

23.
John settles in on the rue Sainte-Anastase

The deep-blue eyes of the old vegetable lady at the street-corner shop twinkled, the wet paint on the neighbouring coach door gleamed, and a spring sun shone down from an azure sky. Craning my neck I could glimpse a tiny patch of sky, but only just, from the window of my flat.

Here I was at last, settled into my new home, the first of my very own, in the rue Sainte-Anastase. Thus far, my life had been as changeable as a weathervane, but now had somewhat stabilized within this tiny space, a base from which I could launch myself towards targets still unknown.

I was starting with a clean slate. I found that the flat was in effect quite bare and scantily furnished, but in the immediate future it held a good deal of potential.

To reach my flat you had to go through a small courtyard and climb the first staircase on the left. And what a staircase it was! It was not one of those endless steep ones leading to a maid's room, but something altogether wider and grander with oaken steps, and it still retained its ancient carved banisters, also in oak. My front door, which was on the first floor, was quite imposing, belying the pokiness of the flat on the other side of the threshold.

As you went in, on the left there was a small bathroom with such a small bath-tub that you could only sit in it, then, up a few steps, you were led into a rather narrow room with an uncarpeted oak floor. There was a tall window on the right that opened inwards, in true French style, and there on the left was the best feature of all: an antique hearth still with its great iron fireback. There was no kitchen as such, but instead there were two hotplates set into a small counter built of bricks in the corner of the room. Turning to the right you went into the sleeping area fitted at the far end with two built-in rudimentary beds, one above the other, just like bunks on a boat. The walls had been roughly replastered and wall-lights brought illumination into what was a rather gloomy room.

The flat had a bare-beamed ceiling, a feature that was all the rage for rented properties in the Paris of that time. "Les poutres apparentes" or "exposed beams" was almost a slogan of the rental market. However, I was not about to paint quotations and proverbs on the beams as Michel de Montaigne had done in his library. Nevertheless, the atmosphere that they evoked, as well as the stillness that surrounded me, conjured an image in my mind of an isolated attic in which one could write a great work of literature.

All the same, I had to find a way of paying the modest rent, and more romantic ideas had to be put to one side. To begin with, I dabbled in teaching English: Jean-Jacques Bodier, a former student at the Berlitz Total Immersion Centre in London, and, later, his two sons, Stéphane and Emmanuel, received conversation lessons from me every Saturday morning in their fine apartment at the tip of the île Saint-Louis. That was an infinitely bigger space than my own.

Jean-Jacques had a good, stable job as director of a firm manufacturing industrial coatings and worked in a small office on the Champs-Elysées. In contrast, besides the teaching, I still only had spells of temporary employment at the bank. All the same, all of this was only short-term work and I needed to find something else more permanent to make ends meet.

There was of course the possibility of doing translation work for agencies. And I did have a go. Yet, putting the instructions for use for domestic heating stoves into English was a long way from the kind of writing that I wanted to do in my attic!

*

Nothing can match the graceful movements of four couples dancing the quadrille. To the lively rhythm of the music, the dancers form squares, with chassés, dos-à-dos and spins.

But for me Quadrille was also a French bulldog, a handsome bitch with sleek coat, belonging to the Bodier family. She moved about a good deal; her moves were jerky, unexpected, though at times sinuous. Her four bow-legs at the corners of her square-shaped body seemed to move independently from each other. Should you be looking for anything rhythmic you would have to make do with the wagging of her docked tail, such as when she welcomed me on my visits to give English lessons to her master. Instead of music there were the overexcited snorts of a dog eagerly greeting you. In short, she was a sort of one-dog band who wanted to be a troupe of cancan dancers at the same time.

My visits became a Saturday morning routine. Once the dog had calmed down, English conversation lessons, accompanied by coffee and croissants, took place in the small dining-room as we sat beneath one of the semi-abstract seaside scenes taken by the photographer John Batho, Jean-Jacques's brother-in-law. A partition wall clad in aluminium sheeting set the room apart from the much more traditional sitting-room with its white marble mantelpiece, its bookcases, its rocking chair, its standing lamp shaped like a cockerel and its carpet-strewn oak floor that creaked at every step you made.

Through the window there was a magnificent view over the Seine towards the quai de Bercy. It was like being on the bridge of a great liner.

Quite often lessons only drew to an end towards lunchtime when Poupette, Jean-Jacques's wife, came home from the primary school where she taught.

*

There was no telephone in my apartment, and I did not want to spend the money with the PTT to rent a line without knowing more precisely if I was going to stay and if I could afford to pay the bills. Fortunately, there was still the pneumatic dispatch service that René had used once before to reach me. You could go to the post office with your letter and for an extra charge you could avail yourself of this service. Your letter was rolled up and put into a special cylinder to be sucked through a tube to another post office for delivery by a postman. It was rather like the system that they used to have in department stores when the saleswoman sent the money and invoice for a purchase to the accounts department by means of compressed-air tubing that ran overhead and through floors to where the cash clerks sat while the customer patiently awaited his change. The pipes of the Parisian pneumatic mail network, however, ran underground through the sewers. The system survived up to 1984.

René Saint-Maur, who had left his job at Richard Nelkène Publicité, was at that time working for *Sélection du Reader's Digest* on the boulevard Saint-Germain. During one of our lunches together, he offered me a short promotional text to translate. This arrived by pneumatic dispatch, with a small sticky label affixed by the postman to my letterbox to let me know in bright red capital letters that an urgent letter had been delivered and was awaiting me within.

The text I was sent was much more like the kind of work that I was looking for. It had an element of literary challenge about it, and for which I would be remunerated! But I had higher aims than this. At the time I was reading Luís Borges's book *Labyrinths* and I was having a go at writing a short story, slightly under the influence of his style, one which, to my mind, was both scholarly and full of irony. The outcome of this was "Flora's Epiphany", a tale about the creative process and automatic writing set in an attic on the île Saint-Louis. I found I was romanticizing the idea of awakening muses through working in a stimulating environment, somewhere rather like my flat.

Maryse at the bank was kind enough to type it up for me, complete with a carbon copy on onionskin paper, and I sent my story to the editorial offices of the *New Yorker*. I could not wait to receive a reply from the magazine and at long last the postman brought me a letter from the United States. They had read my story, and a ready-printed slip with its distinctive *New Yorker* headline, and beneath it the little head-and-shoulder drawing of a top-hatted man with monocle, stated that: "We regret that we are unable to use the enclosed material . . ."

All the same, there was a handwritten request on the message to be sure to send international reply coupons with my next submission.

24.
Provincial doctor to Clive's rescue

One week in late November I knew that I was really feeling under the weather. I normally enjoyed pretty good health, but there was I was with a hacking cough, and my lungs were congested. All my housemates were beginning to worry about me and urged me to go at once to the doctor's surgery in the middle of town. At first, I took no heed, foolishly telling myself that I would soon be better. But I could not shake off the cough. I began to realize that I really should take their advice, and besides, I told myself, it might be interesting to go and see a French doctor and observe how medical services worked on the other side of the Channel.

At the surgery, I had to wait about ten minutes before the door burst open and the doctor strode in to greet me. He was a slim man of average height, nothing very remarkable about him except for his clothes, for he was wearing jodhpurs and mud-bespattered riding boots. He must have been out on horseback.

He sat me down in his office and wasted no time in asking me gently the reasons for my visit. He examined me with his stethoscope and took my blood pressure. He then sat down himself at his desk and scribbled out a prescription, at the same time declaring that my condition was nothing serious but that I should take the medicine he had prescribed.

The pharmacy very quickly dispensed my prescription and armed with my remedy in its small white paper bag I went back to the house. I had often heard tell that the French were overly concerned about the state of their health. And sure enough, when my housemates saw me pulling the two small white cardboard boxes out of the bag, all three of them obviously could not wait to give their opinion on the efficaciousness of their contents.

In the first box that I opened there were some yellow tablets. My friends were quick to explain that these were highly efficacious for dealing with the effects of a liver complaint. Given the richness of the dinners in which we had been indulging, I was convinced that the doctor had got to the root of the problem. However, the contents of the second box rather bewildered me. They were long, transparent capsules filled with liquid. In all innocence I asked my companions how I was supposed to take them.

"Should I pop one in my mouth, swallowing it down with a glass of water?"

They fell about laughing as they explained to me that these capsules were meant to enter the body through another orifice. This was an unusual practice in England, although apparently highly efficacious. But I must admit that I was in no great hurry to try them out!

25.
John meets Luisa

The uneven click-clack of high heels on the oaken staircase, followed by the thud of the downstairs main door as it shut prevented me from enjoying a peaceful lie-in in my new flat. For the first few days I did not know who was making all the clatter, which served as an early-morning call at the beginning of each working day.

Finally, there came the morning when I could no longer contain my curiosity. I half-opened the curtains and through the staircase balustrading caught a brief glimpse of the back of a young woman with long, straight jet-black hair, who was stylishly dressed for work. Next, all her slender figure fleetingly emerged as she negotiated the last step of the stairs on her way into the passageway where the letterboxes were, and then the sound of the main door shutting behind her brought the scene to a close.

"But, who on earth is this woman?" I asked myself. "What does she do for a living?"

A few days later, the riddle was solved.

One late afternoon, I was coming home. As I climbed the staircase, I saw the young woman in question on my landing. She was putting her key into the lock of the small door next to mine. We greeted each other politely. At last, I could see her face. And it was very beautiful, with rounded cheeks, and her black hair merged into the surrounding darkness. Her eyes were smiling as much as her full lips.

"Oh!" I burst out, "We're neighbours then!"

"My name is Luisa, Luisa Amokrane."

As a matter of fact, I had spotted this rather exotic name on one of the letterboxes at the entrance.

"Well, my name's John . . ."

And so began our first conversation and our friendship. Like me, she also worked in a bank. Whereas I worked for a French bank, she was at a large American one, the Citibank on the Champs-Élysées.

From then on, we often had dinner together at the Lutin, the neighbourhood corner bistro where she introduced me to a whole group of her girlfriends from the bank, Lucie among others. I started to feel as though I was part of the Parisian workforce and entirely engulfed in the French-speaking circle.

Luisa owned a VéloSoleX that she parked in the passageway downstairs. This means of transport was much in fashion at that time, but she only used hers to ride at weekends. She could hardly turn up at the office on one of those!

"Listen, John (or Johnny Guitar as she liked to call me), my Solex is always there for you to use. Here's the key. All you need do is fill up the tank from time to time."

I was eager to try this humble but efficient little runabout. Without a thought for the dangers of Paris traffic, I engaged the drive with a pull on the lever and I was off. I loved those trips across Paris, being able to complete my journey more quickly than by car and without the bother of finding a car park. I delighted in being able to scoot down the whole length of the rue du Quatre-Septembre to get back to the Marais without having to stop, for as I went along steadily, the timing was such that I would see the traffic lights at every crossroads change to green just as I reached them. And the petrol for two-stroke engines cost almost nothing.

When Luisa told me about the forthcoming visit of her Swiss

girlfriend, I could not have guessed what my reaction would be when I met her. For sure, I could easily summon up a rather idealistic image of a young woman from the French-speaking part of Switzerland; I had seen so many of them during my year in Geneva, but Jacqueline exceeded all my expectations.

There was a knock at my door. It was Luisa.

"She's here!" she exclaimed: "Come on up and I'll introduce you."

"I'll be straight up," I answered, running my fingers through my hair.

Shortly afterwards I went round to her flat and clambered up the little staircase within.

A beautiful brunette, who was sitting in the only armchair in the flat, rose to her feet and came over to meet me. Slender and tanned, with longish hair, she gave me a smile.

"Hello John, my name is Jacquy."

Luisa looked on approvingly.

Over the few days of her stay in Paris, Jacqueline and I became good friends. We went for long walks: she loved window-shopping under the arcades of the rue de Rivoli, halting more than once to admire some jade bangles or beads she saw in the shop window. I remember buying her a copy of *Peau de chagrin*, the novel I was reading at the time. It must have been to the Galignani bookshop that we went to buy it. I wanted her to share the pleasure I was having in reading Balzac's skilfully told cautionary tale about ambition and yearning.

We sat on my home-made sheepskin rug and drew each other's portraits. She left me a black-and-white studio photograph of herself and asked me to make a drawing from it. After she had gone back home to Switzerland, I can still sense the achievement with which I strode into the post office in the rue Sainte-Anne with an envelope addressed to her at Vevey in the canton of Vaud, containing her photograph and my new pencil drawing that had caught at least something of her likeness, or so I thought.

But what I recall of her visit to Paris was above all her perfume. I had hardly noticed the slight swing of her hips as she walked, or the way her hair had bounced with every step she took. In the pyramid of perfumes, citrous fragrancies are the most fugitive while those of wood essences the most lingering. I do not know which perfume she wore, it wafted indeterminately somewhere between the two, but I must admit that I was bewitched by the complex and enticing aroma the depths of which are sealed in my memory even to this day. In short, the recollection of her fragrance more than anything else brings back the delight and pride that I felt strolling along the streets of Paris, with this beautiful young woman on my arm.

26.
Clive learns his lesson skiing at Cauterets

I had never gone skiing in my life. As a man from the lowlands of East Anglia, I knew precious little about mountainous regions. At least I did know that there were several ski resorts up in the Pyrenees not that far from Salies, and it struck me that as soon as winter came I really ought to make the most of these facilities. From the top of a small hill on the outskirts of Salies, you could get a wonderful view of the ragged mountain skyline of the Pyrenees. There was many a time that I went back up that hill, always awestruck, as I beheld their sheer immensity. By November, as the temperature began to fall, I had noticed that a blanket of snow was now beginning to creep down the flanks of these mountains.

Soon after I got back from my Christmas break in England, early in the New Year, the chance came my way of becoming better acquainted with the Pyrenees. For the benefit of the citizens of Salies, the mayor's office had organized a day trip by coach to the skiing resort of Cauterets in the Hautes-Pyrénées. At long last I would be able to try my hand at swooping down those slopes.

On our arrival we were met with a beautiful sight. Some way off were the steep runs down which skiers, who obviously knew what they were doing, gracefully swooped at high speed. Closer at hand much gentler nursery slopes awaited me as a novice skier.

Once I had been kitted out with boots, skis and sticks from

the hire shop, I cockily thought that I had no need of a skiing instructor. So, there I was all on my own making my first attempt ever to ski downhill. I tentatively pushed down on my ski poles and as I began to move, I tried to follow the manoeuvres and movements of other skiers around me. Luckily enough, I did not fall and as I gathered speed it soon felt as though I was sliding along at a good lick. On these nursery slopes there were no ski lifts provided. When I reached the bottom, somebody kindly told me that the best way to climb back up the slope was crab fashion, walking sideways one ski step at a time. After each descent I climbed back up to an ever higher starting point. My confidence was sky-high. Without a shadow of doubt, I began to get ideas beyond my level of competence, convincing myself that one day for sure a brilliant career as a professional skier lay ahead. There was one snag. In my enthusiasm, I had omitted to practise the vital skill of how to bring myself safely to a halt.

There I was at the highest spot yet, getting myself ready to set off down the nursery run. I pushed off with my two sticks and bursting with confidence I soon found myself hurtling down at breakneck speed. However, speed had gone to my head, and I had forgotten all about the café at the bottom of the slope that stood in my path. All of a sudden, I was gripped with fear as the café grew ominously larger before my eyes. Utterly clueless as to what I should do next, I let go of one of my sticks and with all my strength plunged the other one deep into the snow. There was nothing graceful about what happened next. I found myself performing a series of unplanned somersaults, luckily by this time having shed my skis. The last of these left me stretched out on all fours plonked in front of the sun terrace of the café, which was packed with astonished – and no doubt slightly alarmed – customers.

27.
John's friends find connubial bliss

At almost the same time that I settled into my flat in the Marais, Georges and Sandra found a small apartment at 52 boulevard Beaumarchais, not far from the place de la Bastille. If my small space was that of a bachelor on the threshold of his career, the layout of the Casas's flat was better suited for a newly married couple. Whereas I had started off with a very sparsely furnished flat, the Casases had begun their married life with nothing at all in an apartment that was utterly bare. I had taken on my flat on a temporary basis whilst the Casases had rented theirs as a permanent home for the time during which Georges would be working as a designer in his Paris film workshop.

I remember so well that great moment when all the furniture arrived from Florence. It had all been unloaded on to the wide pavement outside their flat: a dining-table; very fragile ornamental chairs; a bed; a mattress; and glazed Tuscan stoneware and bed-linen in wooden crates. They lived up on the third floor and everything had to be heaved up the staircase, for there was no lift. Sandra was laughing all the time, clearly moved by the presence of all these things which had been freighted in from Italy. Georges did not show his feelings so much but was doubtless glad to see that their flat would soon be properly furnished. I, for my part, found it amusing to see such a Tuscan-style collection momentarily spread out on the pavement of a Paris boulevard. In fact, it was an odd way to become acquainted with Tuscan interior decoration, for at that time I had not yet been to that region. There was something Mediterranean about the colours and shapes, which was in stark contrast with the northern light of Paris.

"Come and have dinner with us this evening," said Georges. "We'll soon have everything straight."

This, the first of many meals at their place, followed the typical Italian formula of pasta, veal and fruit.

"Let me show you round the house," said Georges proudly at the end of the meal.

And there was plenty to be proud of. Everything had been allotted its proper place; it felt comfortable but with a truly southern look to it. In the bedroom, above the bed, Georges had affixed a board from the side of one of the wooden crates, on which was stencilled in bold capitals: "COSMA"; this was Sandra's maiden name. Truffaut's film *Domicile conjugal* came to mind. It really was bed and board!

Over a number of visits to their flat, Sandra and I swapped language lessons. I wanted to follow the system as developed by the Berlitz School, by which you listened to a sentence in the foreign language and then tried to understand what was said through context, without being given any translation or any grammatical explanation.

Whilst doing a short course in teaching English as a foreign language at Berlitz in London, the previous year, I had been given an absolute beginner's lesson in spoken Japanese according to this so called "direct method". The teacher holding up a book asks "*Nan desu ka*?" and the student learns to say what it is: "*Hon desu*." I had been utterly taken by this system, for I had really started to learn Japanese after only one lesson and could subsequently give the very same lesson to whomsoever thereafter – and still can. So, I said to myself, why not do the same thing with English lessons for Sandra, and Italian ones for me?

I cannot forget the silly conversations in elementary Italian that ensued:

"Che cosa è questo? È un portacenere?"

"Non è un portacenere; questo è un bicchiere."

"Ti chiami Sandra?"

"Non mi chiamo Sandra, mi chiamo John."

Sandra made huge progress in French, a little less so in English. Georges, already bilingual in French and Catalan, soon learnt to express himself in Italian, and with relative ease. His desire to make himself understood carried all before it.

28.
Crossing the border into Spain

So carried away was I by my new lifestyle in France that I barely realized that five months had already gone by – and I still had not set foot in Spain.

The town of San Sebastián lay just over the border, and it was in February that I made up my mind to have a change of scene and spend a weekend in Spain. Keen not to waste money on coach or train tickets I thought I would give hitch-hiking a try. After all this was not the biting cold of a gloomy English winter but the balmy weather of the Béarn with its bright light.

On the Friday that I set off, I was relieved to find that there were more than enough car drivers on the road willing to offer me lifts. As we sped through the countryside, I found it hard to believe that it was a winter's day; only the nakedness of the trees told me that it was. Before I knew it, I had reached Hendaye. This was more than just a border town; it was also a popular Atlantic seaside resort, with a magnificent beach stretching away far beyond the frontier.

What a contrast with the Spain that I had wandered through as a 19-year-old! Here the huge breakers crashing on these west-coast beaches had nothing in common with the usually lazy and slow-moving Mediterranean off the beaches of Barcelona and Tarragona. The wind blowing in off the Atlantic was markedly stronger than the sea-breezes that tempered the heat of Spain's eastern seaboard.

Here in the Spanish Basque Country, it was not only the ocean that was churning, for it was patently obvious from the moment I stepped across the border that there was boiling resentment at having to live under Franco's dictatorship. On the road to San Sebastián all the drivers whose cars bore Spanish number-plates wasted no time in telling me that they were Basque and not Spanish. Nevertheless, they were still quite happy to let me chat away with them in Castilian; after all, they could hardly have expected me to be fluent in Basque.

And soon there was my first sight of San Sebastián, a most stylish town meeting the sea in the bay of La Concha, shaped like a scallop shell. To one side of the bay stood the old town, where the locals took their evening stroll. At nightfall, I joined the boisterous throng of people sauntering down its narrow streets. I knew San Sebastián was renowned for its exceptional tapas, and it took little to tempt me to partake of some at several small bars along my way.

Much less appealing was the large and threatening omnipresence of the Guardia Civil, wearing their black *tricornios* or three-cornered hats, and with their green capes wrapped round their shoulders. These olive-green spectres that haunted the squares and street corners seemed only to exude malevolence as they scrutinized the passers-by. They made me feel most disquieted. Nothing could better exemplify the unyielding régime of Franco. I had even seen the man himself with my very own eyes as he was being driven in a state limousine through the Parque del Oeste in Madrid three years before.

As I walked towards the French customs officer on my way home, I felt slightly on edge, but this was for a rather different reason. What was worrying me was that I had stuffed more than the official allowance of Spanish cigarettes into my travel bag. Being a non-smoker none of this was for me, however, but destined for my colleagues back in France. Before I had set off for

Spain, they had inundated me with requests for cigarettes, for everybody knew that tobacco was much cheaper over the border.

"You know what Clive," they said, "French customs don't care a fig about what an Englishman may have in his bag as he walks back into France."

With an unsteady hand, I showed my dark-blue passport to the customs officer. He gave it a cursory glance and swiftly eyed my bag. I waited for what seemed like a very long moment. Then, with a casual wave of his hand, he let me walk through.

Some of the French citizens who were returning home by car did not share my luck. It seemed to me that the customs officers had stored up all their energy and zeal in order to disrupt their fellow countrymen's journeys. I spotted a long line of cars awaiting a thorough inspection by the customs. The officers were subjecting these drivers, one by one, to severe interrogation, insisting on examining the contents of every item of luggage in the boot in their quest for tobacco and alcohol that might be being brought in in illicit quantities.

On my way home the weather was still mild; the sun shone brightly. Safe and sound back in Hendaye, I strolled along the seafront. The ocean lay glinting in the sun; I could not resist taking the few steps down to the beach and walking across the corrugated sand to reach the water's edge. On that day the Atlantic was in benign mood, its waves lapping gently across the sand. And just as I had done so often in childhood by the North Sea, I took off my shoes and socks to go for a paddle. The Atlantic water was much less cold than I had expected. After five minutes of splashing and daydreaming, it was with reluctance that I had to leave the ocean behind to complete the last leg of my journey.

Luck was on my side, for I was picked up by a driver who would be passing through Salies and was thus able to drop me off right outside the picture house.

My colleagues rushed out to meet me the moment they caught

sight of me walking up the drive at Mosquéros; but their gaze instantly switched from me to linger hopefully on my bag. As I pulled out the goods, they whooped for joy, proffering bundles of banknotes for the contraband I had brought back with me from Spain.

29.
John meets Chuchi

When I first met Jennie, she was a bar girl at the Landolt, a student drinking haunt near the old main building of the University of Geneva. A chatty, shapely blonde, she had come over from England and had learnt her very idiomatic Genevan French at the bar. After that, she had become a waitress in a workers' restaurant not far from Cornavin, Geneva's main railway station. Her Genevan accent became still thicker.

One day, the idea came into her head that she should go to Paris for the first time in her life, and so she dropped me a line. I must have met her at the Gare de Lyons and then showed her round some of the sights of Paris. As we came up the escalator at Métro Franklin D. Roosevelt she was stunned by the brilliance of the nightlights stretching away from us along the Champs-Élysées all the way up to the Arc de Triomphe.

"John, could we go the Gare du Nord a bit later on," she asked part way through the evening. "An English friend of mine is coming over for the big England–France rugby match."

"But of course."

We reached the station just in the nick of time as the boat train from Calais rolled in.

"Ah, there he is! And looking the same as per usual."

She rushed over to a young Englishman who was slowly making his way towards us with his luggage.

At exactly the same moment, a young couple was heading to

greet the same young man.

"Let me introduce you to Nigel," said Jennie, opening the conversation.

We shook hands.

"And may I introduce you to Chuchi?" Nigel added.

"And this is Lilian," said Chuchi.

"Why don't we all go for a drink?" I suggested.

Seated in a café on the boulevard de Magenta, we soon learnt all about each other. Chuchi was Turkish and had lived for a few years in London, where he had met Nigel. Lilian was Swedish and just like Chuchi she had signed up for a course at the Alliance française to learn some French.

We all got on very well together. I learnt that Chuchi was looking for a bedsit he could share. I suggested to him that he should come and see my flat with a view to sharing it with me. I could see that this might be the way to cut down my expenses a little and at the same time widen my circle of friends in Paris.

Chuchi came from Trabzon, a port in the far north-east of Turkey, not very far from the border with the Soviet Union, or, to be more precise, with Georgia. He was immensely proud of his origins from among the hazel groves in the hills behind that city. He was my first real contact with somebody from this part of Asia and I found this exoticism intriguing. With his strong facial features, he bore something of a resemblance to Jean-Paul Belmondo. He spoke fluent English but at the time had only a smattering of French. Thanks, though, to his course at the Alliance, supplemented by a few grammar lessons from me, he made huge progress.

I wanted to learn a little Turkish in return, but I was completely flummoxed by the utterly different way of thinking behind the language and the way it was expressed. It is an agglutinative Turkic tongue and one which is graced by a fascinating use of vowel harmony. And without change of pronunciation, Chuchi's own name written in Atatürk's version of the Roman alphabet, becomes Çuçi.

Only much later did I have a fuller picture of his roots. I knew that his family was in the haulage business in Turkey, but I had no idea of the scale of their network of coaches and lorries that covered the whole of Anatolia.

For him, his stay in Paris must have been a short Bohemian interlude!

30.
Clive heads for the metropolis

Living in the Basses-Pyrénées it goes without saying that I was leading a distinctly rural life, but that did not stop me from wanting to experience life in the capital. The opportunity came for me to go to Paris during the February half-term break. My rail ticket was cheap enough thanks to the concessions made available to teachers in the public sector.

Lying on my narrow couchette, the gentle rocking of the train lulled me to sleep. But my mind must still have been whirring with anticipation, for, as I shifted from side to side, I kept on waking up. At last, a grey dawn light began to seep into the wagon; but with the sun obstinately refusing to put in an appearance.

I climbed down from my couchette to have a look outside my compartment. I had the corridor to myself. Out of the window I could see the huge bulk of blocks of flats looming out of the fading gloom of the night, and then the vista of a wide boulevard, and, rushing over to the opposite window, the tracks of a vast goods yard, where the covered wagons were doing their first shunts of the day. And just beyond that, lay the great river itself. The other passengers may well have been sound asleep, but there was no chance of a lie-in for them because, with a screeching of brakes, the train came into the Gare d'Austerlitz.

I found myself on the platform borne along by the luggage-laden throng as it headed towards the entrance to the Métro. I had booked myself a room in a small hotel down one of the streets off the boulevard Saint-Germain. Looking at the Métro map my nearest station was Saint-Germain-des-Prés.

I had heard about the greyness of Paris but stepping out from my hotel onto the rue du Four, there was a burst of brilliant colour: the blinds and the awnings of the baker's, the butcher's and the grocer's had been unfurled in the wan morning sunlight lending them a much more lively look than their London counterparts.

Back at my hotel, I stretched out on my bed for a few minutes, with the shutters and windows closed to keep out the din from the street below. As I awoke, I reached for my watch. It was three o'clock in the afternoon! I could hardly believe it. And my tummy reminded me that I had not eaten a thing all day! I left the hotel and ambled down the boulevard for a small snack, not wanting to spoil my appetite for dinner.

Wandering along the narrow streets of the district that evening, I studied the menus posted outside the restaurants, spoilt for choice as I read their enticing offerings. Following my nose, I went into a bistro by the name of La Boucherie. I pushed open the door and walked into a small, cosy dining-room crammed full of young diners who were devouring their *steak au poivre*, a speciality, so it turned out, of the house. I reckoned that students from the nearby Medical School that I had glimpsed just now were amongst its patrons. I chose the *pâté de campagne* and just like them followed that with a pepper steak washed down with a jug of red wine. I felt very much at ease in these laid-back surroundings, but how much sweeter it would have been had Marianne been there with her lively presence and laughter, our eyes meeting across the table? And yet, as I sat there thinking about her, I began to wonder where exactly our relationship was heading.

Next day, I rose early, and, after a quick breakfast, I set off on a voyage of discovery of the secrets of the capital. The city was already coming to life: shopkeepers were hosing down the pavements outside their shops; the passers-by were hurrying along, no doubt preoccupied with thoughts about the tasks of the coming day.

Lying on one of the straight-planked benches under the bare trees of the square in the rue de Furstemberg there was a tramp oblivious to the time of day. Beneath his coat tossed over him like a blanket he slept on. He was in no hurry. If only the half-empty bottle of red wine by his bench could ease any distressing thoughts that might assail him when he awoke.

Crossing the pont Saint-Michel, I turned my head to the right to behold the medieval magnificence of Notre-Dame cathedral that rose up before me, with its towers and jutting gargoyles, and with its flying buttresses along the bank side. Once I reached the cathedral square, I was far from being the only one to be gaping open-mouthed at the multitude of statues adorning the facade. Reaching the other embankment of the île de la Cité, I could see that strollers had sat down on the quayside to watch the boats go by and to make the most of the sunshine with its first hint of spring warmth. For a good fifteen minutes I sat there with them, wondering where those barges came from and where they were going.

Walking over the pont au Change I ended up in the vast Châtelet square. Going by my map, I saw that the Louvre was not far away, and it struck me that I should balance my culinary experiences with a cultural visit to the museum.

As a tourist I had of course to see the Mona Lisa and the statue of the Venus de Milo! And there too was Géricault's giant painting *The Raft of the Medusa*, a gruesome depiction of the survivors of a shipwreck. I was astounded by the scale of this canvas and that of many other imposing nineteenth-century paintings, and then hurried over to inspect the Ancient Egyptian collection. I had been fascinated by the artefacts and mummies I had seen at the British Museum, and knew that Napoleon had spent time in Egypt, so I was keen to see what Egyptian treasures were on display at the Louvre. After feasting my eyes on a few mummies and cartouches of hieroglyphics, I was suddenly overcome with fatigue and needed to sit down for a while on one of the benches.

Back outside, I caught my breath and soon reached the Jardin des Tuileries. Straight ahead was a small pond where young boys were sailing their model boats under the fond gaze of their mothers or nurses. There were yells of delight whenever a light puff of wind propelled the boats from one side of the pond to the other. The boys would then scuttle around the pond to recover their boats as soon as they reached the far side.

Beyond the pond, the white grit pathway stretched ahead and seemed to reach as far as the Arc de Triomphe on the horizon. I decided to make my way slowly along this path, sitting myself down for five minutes or so on one of those cast-iron green seats that dotted the gardens.

I set off again and after a short while arrived at the other end of the gardens and found myself by an even bigger pond, which lay between the long low buildings of the Orangerie and the Jeu de Paume. Looking ahead of me the Arc de Triomphe still dominated the skyline, but in the foreground, I saw the great gates out of the gardens and through them the endless stream of cars in the place de la Concorde that seemed to be going round and round the ancient Egyptian obelisk from Luxor that stood in the middle of the square.

It was at the gates that I saw several men who had unrolled straw carpets on which they had laid out handbags and wooden carvings for sale. They were all quite young and slim and probably came from West Africa. Nearby stood a man who was also young, slim but fair-haired. He had a somewhat Nordic look about him. He was busy blowing up a large red balloon with a foot pump.

Round his waist was a belt to which were strung a bunch of balloons of every shade imaginable that had already been inflated.

I heard him speaking fluent French as he chatted with the mothers of children who were noisily shouting: "Maman, je veux un ballon!"

Seeing this young man, who I concluded was, just like me, a foreigner in France, I was curious to know how it came about that he had ended up in Paris selling balloons. But he was doing such brisk business that I really did not want to disturb him.

Not long afterwards, the entrance to the Concorde Métro station swallowed me up.

31.
John joins the Paris rag trade

The rue Sainte-Anastase lay on the fringes of the rag-trade district. From the rue de Turenne to the place de la République to the north and as far as rue des Archives to the west, wholesale shops selling finished garments, cloth in bulk, buttons, buckles, knick-knacks, threads and yarns were jumbled up among workshops making shirts, trousers, dresses and evening attire.

Across the way from my flat was a small shirt shop with only enough window-space to display two shirts. It was there that I was able to buy myself a lovely, patterned shirt in pure cotton, even though the shop was officially for wholesalers only. I was from that district, and I lived across the road. So, why not try and see? I walked into the shop and told the salesman where I lived. He sold me the shirt and to my delight even gave me a trade discount!

Every time I came back home, I noticed a small workshop just before you reached the big main door leading onto the court-yard of 16 rue Sainte-Anastase. If I happened to pass by in working hours, I could see that the place was buzzing. Every now and again I had to stop in my tracks while, to a loud jangling of metal, one of the workers wheeled out of the workshop a huge clothes-rack laden with sheepskin coats and bomber jackets on hangers, to be loaded into a van. If I went past at night-time the workshop was silent, with shutters down, and in front of the premises, stood a whole row of big black plastic bags stuffed with offcuts of fur.

Seeing, almost daily, this vast quantity of sheepskin offcuts about to be thrown away was enough to make me feel ill at ease at such wastefulness. One of the bags was half-open and I could not resist pulling out a fine piece of whitish-coloured soft sheepskin. How could they ever think of leaving all this fine fur to the *éboueurs* or bin men? Little by little, I began to think up ways of lessening this awful waste. There was I living in a working-class district surrounded by tailors and seamstresses. Could I not draw on their inspiration to make something myself out of these bits?

It was quite late at night. The street was empty. I was on my way home. I saw the line of bags against the wall. I grabbed one. It weighed more than I had expected. I gripped it more firmly, pressed my courtyard button, pushed open the door and went inside and hastily put down the bag. The door clicked shut behind me. There I was, safe and sound at the foot of the staircase leading to my flat. I braced myself to pick up the bag and climb the stairs.

Once I had cleared a space on my floor, I slowly and gingerly emptied out the contents of the bag. Other than a few cigarette butts and an empty cigarette packet, the contents of the bag were only sheepskin offcuts. There were tiny bits, bigger bits, some in white skin and some in black. There was more than enough here for me to make something.

"And what on earth are you going to do with all that?" asked Chuchi when he came back the following day.

"Well, you know," I answered defensively, "they throw away bagfuls like this every single day. We have got to do something creative with it."

"Oh, but they have already made fine coats and smart jackets out of the fur. It's only rubbish that they are throwing away."

"Wouldn't it be great to stitch some scraps together and make a coat out of them," I exclaimed, no doubt thinking of Joseph's coat of many colours. "Anyway, we could start off by sewing them together to make a rug."

In my mind's eye I was thinking of a fine floor covering which would make the bare oak boards seem a little less stark.

"You can't stitch all that lot by hand," replied Chuchi. "I'll ask Lucie to lend us her electric sewing machine and between us we'll make a couple of rugs!"

And so, the great project got under way. Chuchi brought over the machine. And for my part, I went off down the rue de Turenne in search of a suitably strong thread and appropriate needles for sewing through hides. Maybe even less than two hundred yards from our place there was a spacious shop, the interior of which had hardly altered since the 1930s. The gentleman who served me treated me in a kindly and professional way.

"I am very sorry, sir, but we are wholesalers; we are not in a position to sell you anything retail. But hold on, sir, this box only contains twenty bobbins of thread and this one only fifty needles."

I walked out of the shop with my purchase, bursting with pride that here I was, yet another local craftsman buying his supplies.

Now work began in earnest. I had to lay two pieces with the fur sides facing each other on the sewing machine worktable and move them around so that the machine would sew them together parallel and near to their edges. When I spread out the two pieces, the white fur of one piece abutted the black fur of the other. All I had to do then was trim off the surplus material with shears. I did some more sewing and gradually a large rug in a patchwork of black and white took shape in a totally random way. Day after day, and yard by yard, the rug grew.

When it came to Chuchi having a go, he restricted himself to making his rug all white.

Jean-Jacques happened to call by.

"Wow! This looks great," he said. "What fine workmanship. That must have been hard work!"

He could see that there was a problem with the growing weight of the rug, making it difficult to handle the way the sheepskin passed under the feed dogs; the great downward force had a tendency to drag everything to the floor. It was just as well that I had bought the needles wholesale for a good number of them snapped in spite of the fact that I was making the rug a section at a time.

"What you really need is a Serger sewing machine", Jean-Jacques explained. "It is much sturdier. And when you have finished you ought to give the rugs a lining."

But we persevered with Lucie's machine; and, foolishly, we never did line our rugs.

A few more days and my work was done. I folded it out, ridge by ridge, and spread it on the floor. The room was utterly transformed.

There, before the hearth lay a fine floor covering. How homely it looked. The visual effect it gave was akin to an abstract painting of the interwar period with a strictly limited range of colour. But at the same time, to me with the eye of a Devonian, I saw it as an aerial view of rolling countryside, with ploughed fields and meadows side by side in their winter hues. And turned upside down the seams stood out in a grid of hedgerows, as irregular as those on any Devon hillside.

A few days later, Chuchi had also finished his rug sewn only with white fur scraps.

"I am giving this one to Lucie," he declared as he marched off with it slung over his shoulder.

Mine remained on the apartment floor for the duration of my residence. Today, many years later, it has become a heavy coverlet on my bed.

32.
Live pop music *à la française*

Although I did not know much about popular French music at the beginning of my stay in the Béarn, I could not help but listen to the songs blasting from the juke-box when I was down at the café. More often than not, these French songs touched on all the usual themes: the joy of being young; of falling in love; and the sorrow of being left broken-hearted. Hearing the songs over and over again, the words and phrases slowly sank in.

When I was in London, I had been to a good number of gigs given by top English pop singers at various London clubs, such as the Marquee Club and the Hundred Club to name but two.

Now in France, I wanted to match that by seeing live performances of pop singers singing in French. I was lucky enough to go to a concert given by the Belgian singer Jacques Brel, who was then climbing the French hit-parade and was one of my favourite performers. That April he was on tour round some of the larger cities of France and, as it turned out, was booked for a one-night stand at Pau, so not so very far from us.

There was a ripple of excitement among all of us young teachers at Salies at this news. And, though we could scarcely believe it, there were still tickets available for his concert.

"Clive, just wait till you see him live on stage," Joseph exclaimed. "He puts heart and soul into every one of his songs."

Saturday night came, and there were eight of us piled into in two cars as we sped off to Pau. The auditorium was jam-packed with locals from all over the Béarn. Every last seat had been sold. It was all very well seeing Brel on television but seeing and hearing him live was of another order altogether.

He strode onto the stage and the applause almost brought the roof down. The conductor raised his baton and the music sprang to life; the spotlight shone on Brel's face, highlighting his hollow cheeks.

"Dans le port d'Amsterdam / Y a un marin qui danse . . ."

As he sang about the sailor dancing down by the harbour in Amsterdam, I was entranced by the sheer passion and energy that he put into the song. And throughout the whole concert, as we listened to the controlled articulations of his husky voice, he held us all spellbound.

What an awful tragedy it was that only a few years later at the height of his career he should succumb to lung cancer.

There was another French singer whom I also held in high esteem, Charles Aznavour. Although I never made it to one of his concerts in France, a few years later whilst working in Canada as a French teacher, I was able to see him when he came to Toronto on tour. Without a moment's hesitation, I bought a ticket. The concert hall soon filled up with fans excitedly waiting for him to appear on stage. And what a dramatic entrance it was! All the spotlights were beamed on him. This slightly built man in an impeccable white suit, held a handkerchief aloft in his hand and then, unexpectedly, let it fall to the ground. His was a truly magnetic presence.

All at once we heard the opening lines of the song:

"Tu es la vague, tu es la mer . . ."

Hearing these words where he likens his lover to a wave of the sea, the audience, who were mostly French Canadians, burst into rapturous applause. And so it was that my experience of French culture went on growing, even far beyond the shores of France.

33.
John and the Marais copper-engraver

One of my former colleagues from my eight-month stint at the Berlitz School in London, an Australian of Czech origin, met me in Paris. I already knew that Herman had a strong interest in modern art, and I was not surprised when he had told me that he had an invitation for two to a private view in the Marais.

We agreed to meet and went to the Galerie Genot in the rue Vieille du Temple, a few steps away from the local fire station. We went in through the thick-glass door that set off a tinkling of little bells hanging on the inside of the door. The gallery within was very cramped, and I quickly realized that the way to reach the main exhibition area was down a narrow staircase into the vaults.

A middle-aged fair-haired lady welcomed us very charmingly. This was Huguette, as I found out later, the sister-in-law of the gallery owner.

"If you would like to go downstairs to see the rest of the exhibition," she said authoritatively.

Down below there was a huge crowd! Attention was mainly focused on the few framed contemporary Japanese prints which were hanging on the wall beneath the refurbished vaulting in dressed limestone. In my mind's eye I can still see one of these pictures, executed on quite a big scale, with rolling fields whose rounded forms were effectively defined by the parallel furrows of a plough. Above these graceful stripes there floated in the sky a

Noh mask with a slightly equivocal expression. There were other engravings, each of them displaying highly stylized renderings of nature: forests, rivers, far-off wooded hills below white whisps of mist, patches of colour, at times in the shape of a fan and adorned with abstract Japanese designs; and again and again there was the Noh mask floating eerily in the heavens, sometimes with a crescent moon and tiny clouds alongside.

"That really intrigues you, doesn't it?" It must have been the lady who owned the gallery who was speaking.

"It certainly does. But what technique did the artist use?"

"It's mezzotinting. Come and meet Toru Iwaya, the artist, and his wife Keiko. He will be able to explain how it is done much better than I can."

I already had some notions about engraving, for my father had done quite a few copper engravings, using either a graver or nitric acid or else a combination of both techniques. And with York, we had both paid 100 francs to an engraver in the Marais to be able to try our hand at dry-point and use his hand press to print our own engravings. When it came to mezzotinting, I had only the vaguest idea what that was about.

Toru and Keiko were a very kind and exotic couple. He was spare in build, earnest and talkative; she was tiny, rather shy, quiet but wearing a smile.

"Well," he said in French with a rather marked accent, "mezzotinting is a very slow process. Very, very hard work. You have to work the copper for a long time, you know, with – *nantueka*, how d'you say – a rocker."

"A rocker?"

"Yes, you create a surface that takes the ink by using a rocker that you – how d'you say – rock on the copper plate."

All at once, I felt as though I had been dropped into the midst of artistic Paris: a most welcoming gallery and owner; meeting an artist as he explained his craft, and moreover a Japanese artist.

The romantic notion of having gone back to the School of Paris in the Montparnasse of the 1920s came into my head. It was almost as though I was speaking to Foujita.

We carried on looking round, and as we were leaving the owner said to me: "My name is Marie-Louise. I hope you'll come back when things are quieter. Do you live in Paris?"

"I live on the rue Sainte-Anastase."

"Ah. So, you are just around the corner! Make sure you come back soon."

Only a few days later, I happened to be passing the gallery and pushed open the door that set the bells jangling. Huguette was there and so was Marie-Louise. After going around the show once more I climbed back up the stairs and chatted away with both ladies.

The gallery had only recently been set up by Marie-Louise and her husband Roland. Having taken early retirement for medical reasons from his career as a urology specialist at the spa town of Contrexéville, Roland had come back to Paris and together with his wife had set up this lovely artistic gem of a gallery in the heart of the Marais. Unfortunately, Roland was seriously ill with leg ulcers and in great pain, so I only met him later, when he was feeling a little better. Marie-Louise, a bundle of energy and ideas, ran the gallery. Behind her open face lay an open mind. She was ready to make the gallery into a hub of contemporary art without any preconceived notions, and ready also to take on and show the work of artists who were still unknown. Toru and Keiko Iwaya, who fell into this category and, moreover, lived on the rue Vieille du Temple, almost opposite the gallery, happened to walk in just at that moment.

And so it was that the conversation about mezzotinting was resumed, and soon a friendship with this Japanese couple was forming alongside one with Marie-Louise and Huguette.

Toru invited me to visit his studio, which I did not long

afterwards. I eased open the main door into 41 rue Vieille du Temple and found myself in a small courtyard. Was I about to go into the room of a penniless artist? First of all, I needed to find staircase B at the far end on the right. And, as if by magic, I spotted a little sign at the start of a short corridor that showed the way to this staircase. I stepped forward and climbed up the narrow bare oak stairs with their blue banisters and reached the landing on the fourth floor. There I saw two doors each of which bore the name Iwaya. Which one did I need to knock on? Going for the far one, I tapped on the door and it opened straightaway.

"Ah! John! Do come in, please. Come in and sit down."

I sat down on what I presumed was a bed with cushions around the edge. I looked about me. Shelves laden with reams of paper, engraver's tools, copper plates, and prints stacked between leaves of tissue paper filled the low-lit room. In the middle of the room in a small pool of light stood the printing press and the workbench with notebooks and jottings in Japanese, more copper plates – and a rocker.

I understood right away how he worked. Toru had to cover systematically the surface of the plate with the ridged rocker in order to give the metal a grainy texture that would hold the ink. Then he had to use a scraper and a polisher to highlight areas on the plate that would not hold the ink. There was a separate plate for each colour. Toru started off with the black one. He could only do two hours of rocking per day; this he did to the accompaniment of recordings of Japanese or Western music.

The workshop was tiny, with scarcely room to sit down or welcome guests. But there had to be hospitality all the same, and Keiko came into the room with a lacquer tray containing a pot of Japanese green tea and three cups and put it down on a small table by the bed.

The ceremony began. I was not at all familiar with the way I should behave when drinking Japanese tea and was astonished each time that Keiko and Toru drank a mouthful of liquid, they smacked their lips as they slurped. Keiko said little but smiled and went on noisily sipping her tea.

"Have you known Marie-Louise and Roland for long", asked Toru.

"No, not long, only a few weeks."

"They are very, very kind. And it is very good to have an exhibition in their gallery, isn't it? Selling my prints here is very difficult. But at the Galerie Genot people are beginning to show an interest. Creating a – how d'you say – a market for mezzotints is not easy."

In a torrent of words, Toru told me something about his life: how they had come to Paris from Koriyama in the north of mainland Japan with almost no luggage and with a great deal of determination to study under Stanley William Hayter at his studio, Atelier 17. But Toru must also have seen a few engravings by the Japanese mezzotint artist Yozo Hamaguchi, who had taken up this Western technique whilst in France and had made something utterly Japanese out of it. Toru was bowled over by this method and its enigmatic effect whereby shapes seem to well up out of the dark depths of the picture. Having studied fish-farming at college, Toru had given up what would likely have been a much safer choice of career, given the Japanese propensity for fish, to go in pursuit of a dream that was hard to achieve. A dream, though, that he was able to fulfil step by step so that – much later on – he would become the master of the genre in Japan.

34.
Clive answers the call of the south

Peter, with whom I had spent a day out shooting in the Haute-Garonne, was a good pal. We had got on well from the moment we had arrived at university in London as freshers. Something to do with our age perhaps. I had had two years in the world of work before resuming my studies at the age of twenty. A year and a half older than me, Peter had also worked beforehand. In fact, he was the second oldest student in the class.

I had been over a couple of times to see him that autumn at Montréjeau, and I was delighted to see that he had brought over his Spanish guitar from England. He had rented a room in a building where there was a fishmonger's on the ground floor. There certainly were invasive smells at certain times of the day! The window of his lodgings looked out onto the main street in town, so was ideally situated to keep an eye on all the comings and goings of the townsfolk. I saw straightaway that like me he had swiftly adapted to his new lifestyle, which was a far cry from that of cosmopolitan London. There was not a single café in town where the waiter did not already know what he was going to order as an *apéritif*. No matter which café he went into, there was a small glass of Ricard put on the counter for him in no time at all.

What is more, he had unearthed a local eatery, the Café Restaurant de la Place, which regularly provided him with an evening meal. Every time I came over on a visit, we went there and tucked into copious, but modestly priced dinners. The owner, Madame Lavedan, was a kindly, middle-aged lady, always elegantly attired, who did all she could to make her two young English customers feel at home.

For sure, Peter must have been able to keep his costs low, for I learnt via a postcard that he had squirrelled away enough money, even on his modest earnings, to buy himself what he considered was a smart car, a Simca Aronde – second-hand of course. Carried away by his enthusiasm, he assured me that this was *not* an old banger but a vehicle in good nick which he had snapped up at the very reasonable price of 800 francs.

At the end of April, there came another postcard from him:

> Montréjeau.
> All going well in the Haute-Garonne. I am having fun. Everything is going swimmingly. And the car is behaving itself. I've got an idea for the end-of-May break. What about going on a jaunt round the Languedoc? Do you fancy that? Peter.

A chance to visit the Mediterranean coast was not to be missed, and I shot off a postcard to say "Yes please" by return.

After a few more postcards to and fro, we settled on a date and off I went on the train to Montréjeau. The first thing he did was proudly show me his car parked outside the fishmonger's. I saw that the bodywork did look sound and that it was painted in an olive green.

"Wasn't I lucky? It was dirt cheap," said Peter.

That evening as we walked into his usual restaurant, Madame Lavedan caught sight of me and, recognizing me straightaway, began to tease me: "Ah Monsieur Clive, you're back at long last. It has been a good while. Could it be that you were frightened off by the winter snow that we have in our neck of the woods?"

The next day our voyage of discovery began. There was not much traffic on the road and the car seemed to eat up the miles. While the car engine purred, we chatted away, not so much about work, but rather about our spare-time activities.

"How's the guitar-playing going?" I enquired.

"Oh. Pretty well. You know, I have also been using my guitar in my teaching. The younger ones love to sing along to 'We all live in a yellow submarine'."

This seemed a long way from the Peter I knew as a folk singer. A highly accomplished player and singer, before his stint in France he had been the life and soul of the college folk club in Kingston, which he also ran.

What a lot of catching up we had to do, and how great to chat away in our own tongue again after so long.

Gradually the countryside took on another aspect. We left behind us the green fields and small woods of deciduous trees as we came into an altogether more arid region. Rocky hills rose up on both sides of the road, their flanks dotted with olive trees and dark-green cypresses.

In the Languedoc at that time of year you would have expected a blue sky every day. But on that day the sky was gloomy and threatening, the heavy clouds hovering just above the hilltops. There was a sudden flash of lightning followed a few seconds later by a deafening clap of thunder. Then came more flashes of lightning that crashed into the surrounding hills. It was a truly fearsome storm and although we fully realized that travellers in a car are in a relatively safe place in the event of a storm, our conversation faded away throughout the half hour that the storm lasted.

It was six o'clock in the evening and now the air had markedly cleared. We decided it was high time we found somewhere to stay for the night. As we came round a bend in the road, we drove past the sign for the *commune* of Lavelanet that lay just ahead. Its street was lined with terraced houses with faded grey facades and red-tiled roofs. The sun had come out again and the returning heat only served to increase the sleepy look of the place. Peter was quick to spot a hôtel-restaurant bearing one of those Les Routiers signs affixed to its front wall.

"Well spotted! That's not going to cost us too much," I exclaimed, knowing that this seal of approval, first given to roadhouses catering for lorry drivers, was a guarantee of good-quality food at a fair price. Within the French culinary tradition good food must always be available to travellers of every walk of life.

We were already starving, but to while away the remaining hour until the restaurant opened at seven o'clock, we predictably drank a pastis or two at the bar. When dinner came, we were not disappointed: great hunks of rustic pâté were followed by steaks and mounds of chips. We were intrigued that the waitress had brought us a vast platter on which there were no fewer than four steaks.

"Is this all for us or are there other customers about to join us at our table?" Peter said to the waitress.

"Oh no, sir, all of this is for you to enjoy," she answered with a smile.

We knocked back a bottle of full-bodied red from that region – a Corbières, which went perfectly with our food.

*

Next day, we set off eastwards in glorious sunshine, heading for Narbonne and the Mediterranean coast and then for Canet-Plage. There we were at last with two days ahead of us and nothing to do but enjoy this warm May sunshine. Just the two of us: two young Englishmen – and a French motor car.

But on venturing into the sea at Canet-Plage we found there was still a spring chill to the Mediterranean, and we kept our dips short and sweet. We were dazzled by the southern light, which banished all thoughts of London and of those stuffy lecture theatres waiting to reclaim us come the end of September. Unconcerned by the tensions and worries to come, we were taken by the present moment, its warmth, its light, and the lazy murmurings of the sea.

Far from our gloomier northern existence in England, we were entranced by this sun-drenched way of life in the south of France.

35.
The need to feed the inner man

The Galeries Lafayette department store on the boulevard Haussmann, a stone's throw from my bank, was holding a sale. As the shop's public address system constantly reminded its customers in breathy tones, "Il se passe toujours quelque chose aux Galeries Lafayette", and that catchphrase was true: there was always something happening at the store. Right now, there was the big spring sale. I started off in the kitchenware department down in the basement and came back home laden with parcels. I had bought steel cutlery, glasses, plates, bowls and a small bright red frying pan all at bargain prices. I now had everything I needed by way of equipment to cook myself a meal.

Thus began my great culinary adventure. Without ever wishing to be overambitious, I nevertheless wanted to treat myself to the delicious foods at the market in the nearby rue de Bretagne. Down the full length of the street heaps of vegetables were gleaming, whole chickens were roasting on spits, cheeses were stacked high. To christen my frying pan, I bought two turkey scallops, some onions and green and red peppers and fried these ingredients together in Normandy butter and olive oil.

After this my first success "at the stove", I went back many times to the market to do my shopping, with the sound of the stall-keepers' perennial question for ever ringing in my ears: "Et avec ceci . . . What else would you like?"

And then, when I plucked up courage to ask Ilaria to come

round for dinner, I pulled out my frying pan, and bursting with confidence cooked two fine steaks with fried eggs on top . . .

After Chuchi had moved in, the "banquets" funded by the sale of our balloons kicked off. It was a case of cooking in bulk, but without a full set of kitchen equipment it was tough going. Georges and Sandra came along to the feasts, walking over from their nearby flat on the boulevard Beaumarchais. They have never let me forget a salad I once made out of apples and onions doused with cream. This was a combination that they found very odd, but wasn't it just a Waldorf salad, which I had modified a bit?

If there was not enough time to do the cooking, or if the little greengrocer's shop around the corner was shut, I could fall back on the local eateries. I used to go to Le Lutin with Luisa; or, if there were cause for celebration, I ventured a bit further from my flat to tuck into the delicious steaks served at Chez Robert; and when, later on, there were several occasions when I was kindly invited by Marie-Louise for a so-called "worker's lunch" at the family-run restaurant Au Gamin de Paris. We ate steak there as well, but I reckon that the meat came from the little horsemeat butchers in the rue Vieille du Temple with its great expanse of outside wall to one side on which a rearing red horse was depicted in mosaic tiles; the meat had a texture that was smoother and darker than beef and a rather different but not disagreeable flavour.

One evening when Sandra had observed how much of her pasta I had eaten, she called me "poubelle", the French for dustbin, but I was not alone in tucking in so heartily. The film *The Way We Were*, starring Robert Redford and Barbra Streisand, had just come out and the French-dubbed version of the film was called *Nos Plus Belles Années*, literally "Our finest years". From then on, and without a hint of nostalgia, we called this period of our lives "Nos Poubelles Années".

36.
Clive enjoys good company in the café at Carresse

A short drive down a country lane lined on both sides with fields of maize would take you from Salies to the village of Carresse, a quiet place with houses gathered round the elegant white church. But it did have a café we all liked going to, René, Joseph, Jean-Marie and I. Whenever we felt like slipping away from our town for a couple of quiet hours without having to face a long drive, this village café was a haven for us. It was there, away from the gaze of the nosy townsfolk of Salies and the tales they might spread about our behaviour, that we were able to unwind, giving ourselves over to lively banter and playing cards, with clouds of acrid Gitanes smoke idly floating above our table, and René constantly pressing me to have a glass of Ricard.

It was not all fun and games at the café, for at times the conversation of my French companions drifted towards more serious matters, and I was particularly struck by the great enthusiasm that these my fellow teachers had for the work they were doing and their keen awareness of their pupils' progress. Here I was only in my second year of teaching experience, and the things they said set me wondering if teaching might be the right career for me too. My thoughts turned momentarily to my college in London and to Ron Matthews, as the obvious pleasure he took in his work of instilling in his students an appreciation of French literature and civilization came to my mind.

Monsieur Camy, the café owner, was helped by his daughters

Josiane and Evelyne, both in their late teens. A tall, solemn-faced, taciturn fellow, for ever clad in his blue dungarees, there he would stand behind the bar, for all the world as if he were on sentry duty, keeping an eye on the behaviour of his customers – and of his daughters.

Besides all of us from Mosquéros, there was another young teacher who quite often joined us. From the first time I met him, it was obvious that he shared the same generous spirit and warmth as my other companions. This was Jacques, who taught in a school for children with special needs which lay on the outskirts of Salies. His lodgings were on the other side of town. Nevertheless, he sometimes made his way over to dine with us at Mosquéros. A lad from the Landes with its flat heathlands and wide skies, he was impressed by the rugged countryside around Salies, but, as he once told me, there were times when he felt the surrounding hills were hemming him in, almost crushing him. Yet there had been a time in his life when he had looked down on them from above when he was undergoing military service in the parachute regiment while training at its garrison at nearby Tarbes. Mercifully, he had been spared the trauma of active service in Algeria.

It was always fun having him with us on our evening jaunts to Carresse. And he often joined us on our culinary outings up in the hills, dashing along at speed in his light-green Renault Dauphine, sometimes with me sitting beside him clutching the sides of my seat!

37.
John uses his Métro ticket

The Paris Métro soon became for me a novel form of underground theatre, and each journey an act from a play. When the doors slid open at a station along the way a new scene began as new passengers made their entrances and others on board their exits. Of course, you could never tell who might board the train: sometimes there were tourists, so easily spotted or heard; sometimes commuters, often rather deadpan in expression; and sometimes locals, who went maybe only a stop or two before alighting. The cross-section of passengers varied from one section of the Métro to another. The travellers who clambered aboard with all their luggage at the Gare St Lazare, for instance, were a very cosmopolitan, polyglot bunch. By the time the train had reached Villiers station, however, they were predominantly locals who were boarding. You could witness further subtle shifts in the dramatis personae if you chose to change lines for a train that skirted the eighth arrondissement and took you as far as the Étoile station. If you chose then to board a train that descended into the very smart sixteenth, you would see yet another shift.

Sometimes a beggar came on board and in a sad soliloquy told the story of his life to the whole carriage, after which he systematically made his way down the aisle, rattling a paper cup and pausing hopefully before every likely giver of alms.

On one occasion when a young woman was reading a novel on the train, I peered over her shoulder to see what she was reading. What amused me was that her French novel was divided into short philosophical sections each named sequentially after the stations of another Métro line. I wondered whether each station name was the inspiration for the section it headed, but never found out, for she shut her book and alighted at the next stop.

Every now and again a passenger boarding the train brought into the carriage a lingering whiff of stale garlic.

When working at the bank I always walked to work, so whenever I caught the Métro it was nearly always to go to some form of formal entertainment. I would buy the latest issue of *Pariscope*, one of the what's on weeklies for Paris and scour the films showing listed by district and find the most affordable cinemas to see the latest *drame psychologique* or a thriller by Costa-Gavras or Claude Chabrol. The choice seemed infinite. If it was a foreign film, I checked the list to make sure that the cinema was showing the film I wanted to see in "VO" or *version originale*; I did not like watching films that had been dubbed whether I understood the original language or not. It was not just the challenges of lip synchronization; it was the loss through change of spoken language of a segment of the culture from which the film had sprung. I did, however, go with Henri and some other lads from the hostel to the local cinema to see Sergio Leone's spaghetti western *C'era una volta il West*. Dubbed in French I felt uncomfortable about it, even though we were sitting in deep upholstered seats before a giant screen in the wonderful 1930s Rex cinema on the corner of the boulevard Poissonnière. With its multinational cast, whose mother tongue would have been best? Charlton Heston's or Claudia Cardinale's?

Concerts too were only a Métro ride away. With Georges, I took the train to Ternes, and we attended a breathtaking performance at the Salle Pleyel of Oscar Peterson and Count Basie. There they sat playing to each other at interlocking grand pianos up on stage, both smiling from ear to ear in sheer bliss. And on my own I alighted at Franklin D. Roosevelt Métro station to attend a concert given by the ORTF's national orchestra with Victoria de los Angeles as soloist in that extraordinary Art Déco Théâtre des Champs-Elysées on the avenue Montaigne. She sang wonderfully and with such deep feeling and warmth, and her utterances were clear, but not all the audience was happy. After singing Berlioz's *Nuits d'été* with the hugely evocative romantic words of Théophile Gautier's poems, there were churlish boos from around the auditorium. The only explanation for that must have been that while her voice was beautiful, her pronunciation of the French was slightly Spanish.

The Paris Métro was about to undergo a programme of major improvements. But at that time the modernization of the network had scarcely begun. On some of the lines there still trundled the old green carriages, with their brass door-latches you had to lift before you could slide the doors open, and there were certain seats allocated for pregnant women, the disabled and those with war injuries. This was before the RER [Réseau Express Régional or the fast suburban network] had been completed. At that time, they seemed to be installing many more of those terrifying automatic steel barriers or *portillons automatiques* that seconds before the train came into the station swung shut to stem the flow of passengers boarding the train. It was one of these barriers that had fleetingly hindered Cary Grant as he chased Audrey Hepburn through the Métro in the film *Charade*. For all that, there were still many platform entrances without these gates, where there were still narrow, well-worn metal barriers that swung open when you pushed them. Each of these was manned by a beady-eyed stern woman in a light-blue working coat, who punched a hole in every passenger's ticket.

One evening coming home late from the cinema with Georges and Sandra (we had been to see Fellini's latest film *Amarcord* at a cinema on the Champs-Élysées), we walked on to the platform at Franklin D. Roosevelt station. For whatever reason, the *poinçonneuse* in her blue coat was not there, and her little seat by the barrier was vacant. Georges, spotting the empty seat, decided to sit on it while waiting for the train. Other passengers were coming on to the platform; without thinking, they each tried to give him their ticket. Georges told them, with a beaming smile, that he did not work for the RATP, Paris's public transport system.

On another occasion, in another station, I do not recall which, I went through one of these barriers. Owing to the fact that I was laden with luggage, I had momentarily popped the ticket between my lips. I took it out and handed it to the woman in blue.

"You mustn't do that. Ce n'est pas propre. It's not hygienic!" she snapped scoldingly.

*

The first big change seemed to happen all at once, at least that is how I remember it; my ears were assailed with the swishing sound of pneumatic rubber tyres as one of the fast new trains rolled into the station along its smooth concrete track. This was part of an experiment with technologically advanced rolling-stock being conducted on the two lines forming a giant cross on the Métro map, going from Porte d'Orléans to Porte de Clignancourt and from Étoile to Château de Vincennes. The rapid deceleration of the new cream-coloured rectilinear trains as they came into the station and their acceleration as they departed were accompanied by the soothing sound of their innovative inflated tyres. I fell in love with this brand-new technology as well as with the sleek look of the new carriages, and whenever we went balloon-selling, we loved to ride back and forth from Saint-Paul to the Tuileries on board this new mode of transport.

With the upgrading of the Sceaux line and of other RER lines

I was given yet another thrill, that of being able to travel from the Opéra to the Étoile in a matter of minutes, delighting in the added experience of alighting at the new RER platforms and finding myself in a cavernous underground space that belonged to the future.

How colossal was the contrast between this space-age setting and Hector Guimard's Art Nouveau Métro entrances in cast iron dating from the turn of the twentieth century, with their Métro signs lit up in white on red within a green frame!

As for the tramp I always saw curled up on the grid over the ventilator shaft of the Métro whenever I walked along the broad pavement of the boulevard de la Madeleine, the transport system only afforded him a breath of that warm and musty air from the subterranean comings and goings of others. For him and those like him there had been no change.

38.
Summer festivals – and Clive takes the mike

The very fine June weather had come, and, as in so many villages in the Béarn and in the Basque Country, the townsfolk of Salies had been weeks talking about their *festival estival* that was to take place later that month. There were loads of things to be done: publicity; planning; music for dancing; and, of course, food!

Some of my friends wanted to know if we had similar festivals in England. Indeed we did, I told them, but they were of a very different nature. We had country festivals, I went on to say, that were sometimes bound up with the village church. Some villages carried on the ancient tradition of celebrating the coming of spring by dancing round the maypole, with parishioners selling all manner of local produce at stalls. Other fairs took place up and down the land, but these more often than not were no longer for the purpose of trade as in past centuries but only for amusement. People could unwind and spend their money on a variety of fairground activities: buying knick-knacks; eating candyfloss; riding the dodgems; trying their luck on the coconut shies; and sitting astride the brightly painted wooden horses of the merry-go-round.

As the day of the Salies festival grew nearer, the whole town put its shoulder to the wheel. Lanterns were hung and bunting strung across the square. On the day itself, a wooden stage was erected in one corner. Even from afar you could sense the air of excitement, and when all of us from Mosquéros made our "grand" entrance at about nine o'clock in the evening, we found a square that had been totally transformed. In the lantern light, a throng of dancers swung to the rhythm of the music. The band up on stage filled the whole square and way beyond with the wailing sound of the electric guitar and the loud thudding of drums. People were carousing everwhere, and the café waiters were struggling to serve their thirsty customers fast enough. For sure, it was not just the Salies townsfolk who were having fun: people had flocked in from neighbouring villages. And for them, this was one of the highlights of the season.

From time to time, we caught fleeting glimpses of faces whom we thought we knew, but their features accentuated by the shadows, made it hard for us to be quite sure. Yet even across the teeming crowd I could not mistake the faces of Josiane and Evelyne, the two young sisters from the café at Carresse, as they stood on the far side of the square. And they also spotted us right away and waved. Somehow, they must have been able to slip away from their work and their stern father and mingle with everyone at the festival. We watched them as they made their way over to us. We tried chatting for a while, but soon gave up, for we could hardly hear each other against the loudness of the music. So instead I asked Josiane for a dance and we were soon swept along with all the other dancers. And so the night rolled on. When at last we staggered back home to our lodgings at Mosquéros dawn was breaking.

*

Not that long afterwards, our colleague Jean-Baptiste proudly announced that it was soon the turn of his village down in the Basque country to hold its own summer festival. He invited us all to come along, and after all the fun we had had at Salies, we were more than happy to do so. Late one Saturday afternoon, just a fortnight later, all of us gathered and shot off in several cars heading south for the Pyrenees.

What fine sights and sounds greeted us on our arrival. The place was already buzzing, and the band was playing at full blast. The villagers were ensconced on tiered seating, watching the band. All the men were clad in white trousers and shirts, with red neckerchiefs and their heads topped by festive red berets. Everybody, apart from us, seemed to be speaking Basque. I found it fascinating to listen to the incomprehensible exchanges in their ancient tongue, its origins still swathed in mystery. Jean-Baptiste introduced us to some of his friends, who greeted us warmly, but in French. Ever generous, they were not slow in topping up our glasses as soon as they were drained.

More than a few of them were intrigued to meet me. Even though I had a rather Mediterranean appearance, they must have spotted a slight difference in my gestures and stance. Once I opened my mouth, their suspicions that I was not French were confirmed.

"I've brought an Englishman along tonight!" said Jean-Baptiste proudly.

Nevertheless, I must add that I was far from being the first English speaker to venture into the Basque Country. The presence of the English in the south-west of France was hardly anything new, for as far back as the early nineteenth century, there had been a sizeable, well-heeled English community who would come down to escape the chill of the English winter and to take strolls at Biarritz along the promenade de la Grande Plage, or at Pau along the boulevard des Pyrénées. All the same, I do not suppose that many English ever made it up to this mountain eyrie.

Word soon reached the members of the band that there was a native English speaker in their midst. One of my crowd – almost certainly René – must have told them that I was something of a singer. That was a bit of an exaggeration, though it was true that a few years back, I had been a member of an Anglican church choir and had occasionally sung solo parts in church services. Come what may, the band believed everything René had said about me and there was no way for me to refuse their pleas to sing with them. There was nothing for it but for me to climb up on to the stage and sing my own interpretation of "Puppet on a String", the song that had won first prize at that year's Eurovision song contest.

For a variety of reasons, my memories of how well I sang that evening are rather blurred, but I do recall the enthusiasm of my Basque audience in the level of its applause.

39.
John and the Irishman

There was a knock on the door, the brass door-handle turned and a short young man, with rosy cheeks and wearing a tweed overcoat, came into my office at the BFCE.

"I would like to see Mr John Adamson," he said in English with a soft lilt.

I was sitting not so far from the door and could hear what he was saying.

"That's me," I said, rising to my feet and going over to meet him. "What can I do for you?"

"Well, my name is Patrick Currivan, and I am a colleague of your brother's at the computing laboratory at St Andrews. You could say, one of his friends, and when I told him that I was going to Paris with my parents, he told me that I should drop by and say hello."

Right then was not the best time to hold a conversation, but I wanted to welcome him courteously. There were urgent translations piling up and we all had a lot of work to do that day.

"Delighted to meet you, Patrick," I replied. "I am rather busy right now, but why not come back towards the end of the afternoon and we'll go for a drink somewhere. Do you know Paris at all?"

"Not very well."

"All right then, I'll show you something of my Paris and take you out to dinner."

We set a time to meet, but I do not remember where. Most probably it was at one of the nearby bars on the boulevard.

That evening, Patrick left his parents to their own devices so that he could spend the evening with me. He must have travelled by rail from Scotland to Paris and his folks must have flown in from Dublin to meet him. I was a bit worried that the conversation between us might be awkward, for he was a scientist and came from the world of programmers, about which I knew little. What would we have in common? Then again, he was a friend of my brother's, whose interests went far beyond the realms of science. I hoped it would be like that with Patrick.

Oh, if only I could remember a little bit more about our discussions that evening. All I know is that I was amazed from the outset by his Irish gift of the gab and the ease with which he was able to speak on any topic. We took the big riverboat run by the Bateaux-Mouches company to soak up a bit of the night-time atmosphere of the city. Sitting right at the prow below the bridge, we had a spectacular view that was constantly changing as the boat went up the river. The ship's searchlights lit up the quayside buildings and we laughed when we found that we shared the same hankering for a large artist's studio of our own overlooking the Seine, each with a vast picture window facing north.

I often took visiting friends for a meal at the Vagenende, a fine brasserie on the boulevard Saint-Germain. My cousin Kathy and her husband, Clive Fairchild, on their Paris honeymoon, had been very impressed when I had bidden them there for an evening of gastronomy. Neither of them had ever been to Paris before and so saw everything with eyes as wide as saucers. Founded by the Chartier brothers, the Vagenende was bound to please them, I had thought, since they had so loved dining in the turn-of-the-century surroundings of Le Chartier on the rue du Faubourg-Montmartre. A highly ornate Art Nouveau restaurant, with its small tables, starched linen and attentive waiters, the Vagenende encapsulated to my mind a certain Parisian way of life that I had wanted to share with them.

By way of an introduction to this continental style I took Patrick there too, and we both followed the moderately priced set menu washed down with a glass each of Gewurztraminer. We talked endlessly, with Patrick expressing increasingly original and unexpected viewpoints on a wide range of topics. On the great loom of conversation, he wove the finest Irish twill: resilient in argument and diagonal in approach.

And then I began to hear strains of music and knew that the Ukrainian accordionist had come, as was his wont every evening. Out of the corner of my eye I saw that he had already begun going up and down the lanes between the tables. He was wearing his florid embroidered waistcoat.

As always, whenever he went past my table, I would ask him almost ritualistically to sing "Otchi Tchorniya" and the restaurant would be filled with this passionate and rhythmic music that called to mind the Great Steppes. In his bass voice, deep like Boris Godonov's, he clearly uttered the vowels and consonants while his instrument elaborated on the melodies in rippling arpeggios.

"Let me buy you a nightcap somewhere," suggested Patrick when the music had died down.

"Yes, why not," I said. "I spotted an Irish bar earlier on, not far from here. It's called Kerrigan's or something like that."

Yes, at that time, where the rue de l'Odéon and the rue Condé divide, there was a bar with an Irish name. We went inside. We should have had a glass of Paddy whiskey, I suppose, but we stayed in French mode and ordered two glasses of vintage cognac. We went on chatting a long time. Patrick spoke about his hopes to gain business experience in the world of computing. Working in the United Kingdom and coming from the Emerald Isle, which in mock Irish parlance he neatly dubbed, "off-shore, off-shore

Europe", it was time to seek pastures new and mainland Europe seemed to be beckoning. As for me, I talked about my experiences in Paris in the worlds of film, banking and writing, and sketched out my plans for the future. Quite recently, I told him, I had had an interview in London with Cambridge University Press, the publishing arm of the University of Cambridge. I was awaiting further news. Would they be taking me on as a graduate trainee for their six-month apprenticeship programme covering all aspects of the publishing process?

Ever since the age of five I had been fascinated by how books were made. My father's Puffin Picture Book on printing had long ago caught my imagination. It could be that I might be able to set out professionally in this field, and after spending my six months with such a respected publisher, could more easily apply for a post with another publishing house.

By then we were back in the street, heading downhill towards the Odéon Métro station. Two young women were walking past us in the opposite direction on the same pavement.

"Oh! Comme il est petit!" exclaimed one of them.

It was just as well that Patrick did not understand what she had said. The truth was he was not very tall, but nevertheless had a striking bearing and a finely shaped nose.

"I do like your lifestyle," Patrick concluded, as we came up to the Métro Odéon entrance on the bustling boulevard.

"You know what, John. I have made up my mind: I want to come and work in Paris for a computer firm."

This thought had brought a little colour to his cheeks.

He went off to his hotel and I to my tiny flat in the Marais. We stayed in touch and a few months later he wrote to me to say that he had been able to find a job in Paris working for Bull as a writer of English-language manuals for financial software. In the meantime, I had received a letter from Cambridge University Press telling me that I had been chosen, together with one other candidate, to join its publishing traineeship programme, and asking me when I would be able to start work at its London office.

It was agreed that I would start in early October. By chance this date was more or less the same as the date that Patrick was to take up employment in Paris. Finding somewhere to live in Paris was not easy, especially for a newly arrived young foreigner. So, I suggested to Patrick that he should take over my flat and sort things out with Olivier, the owner, regarding the change of tenancy.

Early in October, I quietly slipped away, handing over the key to Patrick, who moved into 16 rue Sainte-Anastase. When Olivier learnt what had happened, he was not at all happy. But one thing was for sure, Patrick was able to establish himself as my successor, for not only did he stay a long time in that apartment, he was also able to buy one of the third-floor apartments in the same building when Olivier decided to leave for Canada to buy a skyscraper.

For a good number of years 16 rue Sainte-Anastase was a handy bolt-hole for me whenever I visited Paris. It was also an opportunity for me to see how this beguiling Irishman was adapting to French ways and was learning the French language, after his own particular manner.

On one of my trips to Paris, not that long after I had left to work in London, I once more found myself in Patrick's flat. He was sitting there with that afternoon's *Le Monde* newspaper, steadfastly holding it open with both hands, as he attempted to immerse himself fully into the French-speaking world.

I can no longer recall what I could have said to him, but his deep-blue eyes fixed me with a penetrating look.

"Goodness," I exclaimed, "you have almost got the Svengali look!"

"What? Who on earth is Svengali?" he shot back.

I explained that I was referring to a character in *Trilby*, one of

George du Maurier's novels, who had the gift of being able to hypnotize people, and whose hypnotic stare had enabled the young woman Trilby to become a great Paris singer.

"How unfair the world is," said Patrick with a wry smile. "How is it that scientists need to know about literary allusions, whereas all the literary types can go through their whole lives in total and blissful ignorance of the sciences?"

*

John fell silent and swallowed, for remembrances of the words and music of the deeply moving memorial service that an Irish girl called Denise Phelan had arranged for Patrick at the Sainte-Trinité church had sprung to his mind. He remembered doing one of the readings: from a letter of Saint Paul to the Thessalonians. Sitting in rows before him as he stood at the lectern were the bereaved: family, friends and acquaintances, and a sea of grey-suited, grieving colleagues from Euronext. Patrick had died a few weeks earlier in the terrorist attack at Ground Zero in New York.

40.
Small-town wedding

There was a young woman called Murielle who worked as a primary school teacher in Salies. I did not know her all that well, but she was a longstanding friend of some of the teachers at my school. Whenever we gathered on the terrace of the Blason café, and she happened to pass by, she would nearly always stop for a drink with us and join in the discussions about recent happenings in the community.

One late winter's day she told us that she had become engaged and that her wedding would be taking place in May. She was more than generous in extending an invitation to us all to come not just to attend the marriage ceremony but also to come to the wedding reception.

I had not been to a wedding anywhere for quite some time and began thinking about the form of ceremony as it was conducted in England. Couples could opt for either a civil or religious ceremony. Then again, in those days, I believe that the religious ceremony was the more popular of the two.

When I saw the guests arriving at the *mairie* or town hall of Salies on the day of the wedding, I dashed over to join them as they filed inside. I was borne along by this talkative throng as it made its way towards the main room in the building. Over the heads of the crowd I suddenly caught a glimpse of the back of Murielle's veiled head and of Jean, her bridegroom, beside her as they stood awaiting the mayor. Draped on the back wall before them was the tricolour.

We did not have to wait very long before the mayor's office door opened and out came the mayor himself, sporting a wide tricolour sash across his chest. He invited the newly-weds to come forward and sign the papers lying on the large table in front of him.

We then all filed out of the *mairie*, and I made a beeline for the community hall, keen to tuck into the wedding breakfast. I felt sure that there would be some marvellous local food and wine laid on for us. But suddenly, I had the odd feeling that I was the only one heading that way. I looked round and saw that the newly-weds and their guests were slowly walking in the other direction.

"What on earth are all the others up to," I wondered. "Aren't they coming to the banquet? I don't know about anyone else, but I am dying of hunger."

I had thought that the wedding contract was now signed and sealed, but then it dawned on me that all the guests were heading towards the nearby Catholic church of Saint-Vincent. This unexpected detour surprised me, but I dashed over to join them as they climbed the hill towards the church. On the way there, one of the guests who had spotted my confusion told me more about the civil ceremony that had just taken place.

"In France, it is only the civil marriage which has legal standing. The marriage in a church we are about to witness is optional in the eyes of the state."

Gathered together in the church, we witnessed the bride's progress down the aisle towards the priest, who stood at the foot of the steps leading to the high altar. To one side stood Jean, looking very smart as he awaited his bride. Then came prayers, a homily, and finally they made their vows. Whereupon the congregation burst into wild applause.

I could not help myself thinking what it would be like for me to be in the bridegroom's shoes with a French bride at my side. What would it be like if it were Marianne in her white gown walking gracefully down the aisle to marry me? Was I that committed to her? Or were my feelings for her beginning to ebb away?

I could now see that they really did things differently here. For a start, the civil ceremony was compulsory because in France Church and State had been legally separated since 1905. In Britain, on the other hand, the reigning monarch is still both head of State and head of the Anglican Church.

At long last, we were at the community hall, and the feast could now begin. This was truly a great occasion! And for sure there would be delicious food in store for us! Everybody sat at whichever table they wished and chatted away freely.

And then the waiters began to bring in the food.

What a contrast there was between the proceedings here and what sometimes happened at English weddings! There the wedding breakfast could sometimes seem strait-laced, a rather cold affair with the guests seated according to the whim of their hosts. There would be no guarantee of finding yourself sitting with friends or family members. You might just as easily end up sitting with guests you barely knew, if at all.

The consequence of that was that conversation could sometimes be stilted and after the usual polite exchanges, the whole table would often lapse into an embarrassing silence. Nobody would dare bring up such potentially divisive topics as politics, let alone religion. All that was forbidden territory. Many a time you had to spend an eternity stuck at your table while pretending to listen to rambling speeches by the bride's father and then by the groom and finally to the joke-laden speech of the best man. Only when all of that was over could guests break free and mingle with those they wanted to talk to.

At Murielle's wedding feast things were distinctly more relaxed:

all her guests were at liberty to wander around and change places so that they could natter and laugh with their friends. Of course, much table talk revolved around the fine quality of what we were eating and drinking! The roast guinea fowl and the locally made ewe's-milk cheese were washed down with a red Graves from Bordeaux and the desserts came with a Jurançon doux, a local white wine. Not a thing was spared - and there was champagne galore.

41.
John afloat in Paris

A Devon boy must always be within easy reach of water. Born by the river Exe that rises among the heaths of Exmoor and brought up little more than a stone's throw from the Exe estuary, I have always felt I needed to be near the water. Many were the times we went as a family to sandy Exmouth for a bathe, many were the times we clattered along the pebble beach at Budleigh Salterton to go and see the beetling red sandstone cliffs! And on those walks I would often think of the time when the artist Millais had stayed in a house near that pebbly shore to paint *The Boyhood of Raleigh*. I would picture the scene of Walter (another Devon boy from another Elizabethan age) with his brother listening spell-bound to wondrous tales being told to them by a sailor as he points energetically to lands and seas beyond the horizon.

True enough, the river Seine as it flows past the île de la Cité between sheer man-made cliffs of white stone blocks went some way to fulfil my need, and the boats ploughing through the choppy waters stood in for the white horses sometimes encountered at a windy high tide on the Devon coast.

All the same, you could not go swimming in this river. The lifebuoys hanging along the embankment gave warning of the risk of drowning. The water was swift, murky and perilous.

Yet, back then, you could always enjoy that wonderful sensation of swimming outdoors in the very heart of the city, for there was still the Piscine Deligny. Built in wood, this open-air swimming pool floated in the Seine and was moored alongside the quai Anatole-France below the very spot where the boulevard Saint-Germain ends. During the summer months, the swimming pool was home to swimming enthusiasts who loved having a dip or lounging on deckchairs, all without even having to leave the middle of Paris.

Before I did my few lengths, I could glimpse from the upper deck above the changing cubicles the rooftop of the Orangerie across the Seine, rising above the trees, and, if I looked the other way, the Corinthian columns of the National Assembly. As I lay on my back in the water, it was hard to tell whether I was swimming at the same level as the river. Nevertheless, I rather had that dreamlike feeling that I was floating, if not gliding, above the Seine. As I climbed up the small steps out of the pool after my swim, the buzz of the water in my ears turned into the hubbub of passing traffic on the pont de la Concorde.

Going back to the nineteenth century pretty much in the form as I knew it, the Deligny pool was certainly very old, and swimming there it felt as though that great heyday of the lido from the inter-war years lived on.

Then, one day long after I had left the city, the Piscine Deligny was no more – and today there is not even the slightest trace of it. Apparently, at dawn one summer morning in 1993, the swimming pool sank within forty-five minutes to the muddy bottom of the Seine, in a tangle of struts and straiks. The river flows on beneath the Concorde bridge but sadly no longer laps the barge upon which the pool was built.

42.
Clive goes under at Saint-Jean-de-Luz

Living in Salies de Béarn I was only some forty miles from the Atlantic, and in summer months towards the end of the school year a bunch of us often went over there. This was not remotely like my Essex estuary, for the Atlantic Ocean's mood could alter at any moment.

We mostly went to the golden beaches of Biarritz, but every now and again we sought out the less crowded and quieter beaches of Cap Breton or Hossegor. Imagine what it was like: stretched out on the beach; idle days; light chit-chat; no thoughts of my college friends back home in the midst of end-of-year exams. Even René refrained from talking politics or philosophy as we lay there; that would have spoilt our sense of well-being. With our eyes closed we sunbathed, with the sound of the surf in our ears.

My mind wandered to thoughts of Marianne. Soon I would be heading back to London and to two more years' study. How was I going to be able to concentrate on my work with my mind full of that lovely girl so far away in Toulouse? And, if she were thinking of me, how would she cope with her own studies? We were both still so young, and could we really make any kind of deeper commitment to each other? My feelings for Marianne and my fondness of the French way of life had grown enormously over my months in the south-west. But would our relationship withstand the imminent long separation, and would I really want to end up settling in France?

Our state of contemplation was at times broken by one or other of us, who, fed up with all this lounging about, would challenge the rest of us to a swimming race. We would all leap to our feet in a flash, hurl ourselves into the ocean for all the world like a team of lifesavers rushing out to rescue some poor soul who was drowning.

After all this exertion we would collapse onto our towels utterly exhausted. We never needed to leave the beach in search of a restaurant, for we always made sure we had our provisions with us: some cheese-and-ham baguettes and more than enough beer to quench our thirst.

The town I liked best on the Basque coast was Saint-Jean-de-Luz, well known for its fishing industry and justifiably proud of its cultural heritage. It was there in 1660 that Louis XIV married the Infanta Maria Teresa at the church of Saint-Jean-Baptiste. What a wealth of gastronomic delights awaited you in the town's restaurants, offering such an array of fish and seafood dishes. I usually went over there on a weekday, but it was always on my own because my colleagues were shackled to a much heavier workload than mine.

Whenever I went there, I would hitch a lift and it never seemed to take very long before the next car would stop to pick me up. People seemed less suspicious of strangers then.

Always mad about swimming, little wonder that I had just taken up snorkel diving, and there in the horseshoe-shaped bay at Saint-Jean-de-Luz I practised my new aquatic skill. Peering through my mask, visibility in the clear green water was so good that I could see right down to the sandy bed and to a forest of seaweed swaying among the rocks.

Having taken a deep breath, I loved to drop down into this mysterious silent world. I followed a trail through a canyon of rocks admiring the shoals of fish, their silver scales caught for a split second in the shafts of sunlight that pierced the sea. Busy grazing in the midst of their field of seaweed, they paid little heed to me. In truth, I could have drifted for ever in this silent world. And many were the times when I had to resurface speedily for air because I had misjudged the amount of oxygen left in my lungs.

From the green depths of the ocean my head emerged, and as I swam towards the beach my vision was now filled with the soaring green heights of the Pyrenees.

However, not all experiences to do with the ocean were so pleasant. One day at Biarritz I went for a swim. There was a moderate swell to the ocean, the weather was fair, the sky was blue. A light breeze was blowing; the green flag by the lifeguards' station was flapping feebly. I swam out beyond the breaking surf and trod water, enjoying the switchback ride as the waves rushed towards the shore. After a good quarter of an hour, I set off back to the beach doing a gentle front crawl, my mind elsewhere. Only a few strokes away from the safety of *terra firma* my attacker leapt on me. A huge breaker had come from nowhere. A great green wall of water was crashing on me with irresistible force. Buffeted and churned about, there was little I could do. Its energy dissipated, the water drew back and left me, dazed and breathless, tossed onto the sand like a piece of jetsam. Had the undertow been a little stronger, things might have ended rather differently. The ocean was not to be trusted.

43.
John working with the Galerie Genot

It was quite early on in our friendship that I had suggested to Marie-Louise the idea of putting on an exhibition of humorous drawings. To my mind the vaulted space downstairs at the Galerie Genot would be a perfect setting for the intimacy of small drawings. This had already been borne out by the inclusion alongside the engravings of Toru Iwaya of some exquisite drawings by Pascal Vinardel, a young artist born in Casablanca, who had brought with him a subtle understanding of the play of light and shade in his studies drawn in Indian ink.

Now, my father was also a draughtsman, very often working in a humoristic vein, but likewise as an illustrator of books and magazines, and I had wanted to find a way of exhibiting his drawings in Paris. This was something that I had promised him I would look into. I was not expecting there to be a one-man show of his work and so suggested to Marie-Louise that we should bring together a whole range of humorous drawings by artists from Great Britain. I knew that through my father I could readily approach quite a number of artists from *Punch*, *Private Eye* and other magazines.

In her great wisdom, she came up with another idea: to keep things on an even keel, why not also show a whole array of French artists familiar to the French public? And so, the idea of an exhibition of contemporary French and British humour came about with participants from both sides of the Channel. We shared an ignorance of each other's artists. I did know, but only just, the drawings of Piem, and Marie-Louise for her part, those of Quentin Blake as book illustrator.

"All right then," she said. "I'll have a chat with Roland. I think he will leap at the idea."

"Fine," I answered. "Let's speak again once you have had the chance to discuss it with Roland. Goodbye, Marie-Louise; goodbye Huguette."

The little bells behind the door tinkled.

A few days later, I was back in the gallery.

"Hello, John. I have some very good news. Roland is all for mounting the exhibition."

"Well, that's wonderful, Marie-Louise," I exclaimed. "When do you think you would put on this show?"

"Well, there's going to be the Derbré show that I am putting on at the beginning of the summer. Do you know this sculptor? Say we look at a date in the autumn, will there be enough time to do things properly? What do you think?"

"That's a bit tight, it seems to me," I said, "but if I set about writing to the artists in England right away . . ."

"I'll deal with the French artists, of course."

"OK."

Over the following weeks, I often popped into the gallery. I started off by writing to those artists whose addresses were known by my father, typing away on a little Hermes typewriter in sea-foam green belonging to Marie-Louise.

Huguette was usually there, and we enjoyed having long conversations. She talked about life in Paris under the German occupation, about the invasion of young men, many of whom were dashing and attractive, yet they were still the enemy. She was also a gifted teacher and thanks to her I can always spell the rue Vieille du Temple correctly.

"To help you remember the right spelling, don't forget that

the word 'vieille' is like an old man because the letter e stands between crutches."

Marie-Louise was caught up with all the preparations for the Louis Derbré show. I must confess that initially I was not familiar with his work. But some years later I readily recognized *La Terre*, his sculpture made of bronze that had recently been installed in the place des Reflets, not far at all from the Arche de la Défense. This was a copy of his installation in Ikebukuro Square, Tokyo. The subject was a man and woman, both their bodies arched backwards and with their feet, arms and foreheads all touching to form a sphere. On more than one occasion, my visit to the gallery coincided with Derbré's. He had been doing preliminary work on *La Terre* when I first met him. He was a thick-set fellow of medium height, of farming stock from the Mayenne. He had a charming way with him, an open-mindedness, and he did not mince his words. His sculpture *La Terre* struck me as being truly impressive. Yet I did not care for it. There was something about the structure of the limbs which did not seem quite right. Maybe I was looking at the sculpture from a classical standpoint. I much more readily appreciated the lively and carefully studied shape of the running kitten carved by an unknown hand in white stone that Marie-Louise sometimes used as a door-stop.

Only much later did I come to understand the symbolism of *La Terre* and what lay behind this artistic creation plonked in an urban setting.

A very much smaller version of it in polished bronze has been installed permanently in La Coupole on the boulevard Montparnasse, a brasserie where I loved eating on later trips to Paris. This sculpture had been erected to mark the seventieth anniversary of the restaurant. In the course of one of my meals there, I could not help but notice its astonishing shape, then still gleaming in splendour under the chandeliers, but nowadays dull with verdigris. That was one of those infrequent times when I had taken the trouble to book a table by telephone. When we got to the restaurant, the waiter in charge of reservations asked me my name.

"There is a table for two booked for Monsieur Adamson."

"Ah, yes, Monsieur d'Alençon," he replied, glancing down the guest list. "Welcome, your table is this way. Si vous voulez bien me suivre; if you would kindly follow me, please!"

Whereas preparations for the Derbré show were speeding along, those for the humorous art exhibition were not budging at all. I had written to several artists in England on the gallery's behalf, without mentioning either my name or my father's. My letters were greeted with a stony silence. Not even a word. How on earth could we shake up these artists in England? I soon found a very simple and effective solution by starting off with Bernard Handelsman, the American humorous artist who worked both for the *New Yorker* and for *Punch* and who at that time was living in Surrey. I wrote to him in my own name and explained how I was in the middle of setting up an exhibition with the Galerie Genot on humorous drawing. Might he be interested in this idea, and would he be willing to send us a few drawings for sale?

We had a reply almost by return of post. "Ahah," said the letter, "now I understand how the use of English in the first letter from the Gallery had been so perfect. And you are the son of George Adamson, an artist whom I greatly admire. But of course, I would be delighted to take part in the exhibition."

After having sent out a letter that I typed above my own signature and in which I made mention of the fact that already Handelsman and my father had accepted, all the other artists to whom I wrote took up the offer. British honour had been saved.

Meanwhile Marie-Louise had successfully made contact with the French artists.

Almost at once, there was a steady stream of humorous drawings that started to arrive. They came in bundles straight to the gallery from the artists' studios. We left it up to them as to which pictures they would send. It soon became clear that there were too many pictures for the space available. Marie-Louise unearthed a young local picture-framer who made fine but simple wooden frames. They were plain and came at a very reasonable price. Marie-Louise put in an order for a large number made to measure. As for those drawings that were not to be framed, she decided to protect them with transparent coverings in folders on easels for visitors to browse through.

At the outset of our business collaboration, Roland lay bed-ridden in their flat in the sixteenth district. He was home alone while Marie-Louise drove across Paris every day in their little red Renault to put in long hours at the gallery. Then one day Marie-Louise announced that Roland had moved into the gallery. A private area had been fitted out on the ground floor with a daybed and, crucially, a good supply of books. In that way Roland could enjoy a bit of company from his wife during the day, and even if he was not quite in the thick of things, he was at least in the wings. Psychologically speaking, this clever idea was hugely successful.

Marie-Louise told me a year or so later of the highly enjoyable reading sessions she and Roland had had of an evening when he was bedridden in their flat. Sometimes they would choose a novel to read to each other (Marie-Lousie was fond of Marguerite Yourcenar's writings and gave me a copy of *Mémoires d'Hadrien*); sometimes they would choose an art book to browse through together. One evening, she told me, it was the turn of a book on Van Gogh's paintings that they had bought many years earlier from one of the second-hand dealers or *bouquinistes* who plied their trade in all manner of books and old magazines from their dull-green lock-up stalls on each side of the Seine.

As she pulled the book off the shelf, "out dropped a sheet of paper folded in two," she said. Out of curiosity she unfolded it and saw that it was a letter that began "Mon cher ami Gauguin". A mention of a painting of sunflowers with a yellow background leapt off the page, and reading on she found herself drawn into an artist's thoughts on the colours to use for the sitter's hands in a portrait he was painting. At the foot of the letter it was signed "Vincent" . . .

"Would you like to see the letter?" Marie-Louise asked me as she finished telling the story.

"Yes please!"

I met her some days later at the gallery and she carefully brought out the letter from a folder. It was just as she had described it; a sheet with squared feint lines folded in half to make four sides, each filled in neat handwriting. I felt a shiver of excitement as I held what looked as though it must indeed have been a letter in French from Van Gogh to Gauguin.

"I have to go to Amsterdam fairly soon for my job at Cambridge University Press," I said. "If you like, I can take a photocopy along to the Van Gogh Museum there and see what the experts think."

Some weeks later I strode purposefully to the front desk at the Van Gogh Museum and told the receptionist that I had a photocopy of a letter I believed had been written by Van Gogh to Gauguin. A curator was summoned forthwith from his office and within minutes an enthusiastic young man was at my side scrutinizing the photocopies of the two sides.

"Yes, I think the letter might well be genuine. We knew it must have existed," he announced with a slight tremor in his voice. "The letters from Gauguin that came immediately before it are still extant; and this part of the correspondence was missing."

There was a moment's hesitation before he blurted out, "Is it for sale?"

Within days, Marie-Louise told me, the curator was on the train to Paris to inspect the original at the Galerie Genot. But the letter did not end up in the archives of the museum; rather it was sold at auction in Paris and is now in the Musée Réattu at Arles, the Provençal town where the artist had penned the letter and where he had painted some of his greatest masterpieces.

Roland was to regain his energy and was able to walk about a bit and for a while live a fairly normal life. Together with him and Marie-Louise I once went to dinner at the brasserie at La Closerie des Lilas in Montparnasse, and once even to the Brasserie Lipp. For Roland, I think these outings were a kind of nostalgic crusade.

On one occasion we went to the tiny Théâtre de la Huchette to see an intimate production of Ionesco's *The Bald Prima Donna*. The stock phrase "Quelle coincidence bizarre" – What a strange coincidence, uttered several times in the course of the play to underline how absurd things were, became a standard joke in our conversations. As a matter of fact, Roland had a huge sense of humour and often saw the funny side in everyday situations. He was crazy about word games and the origins of words. And it was thanks to him and Marie-Louise that I own the dictionary published by Larousse on the roots of European languages, an extraordinary book that demonstrates the shared origins in both Latin and Germanic languages of words going back beyond Sanskrit into the obscurity of a former Indo-European tongue. I remain convinced that this blend of humour and curiosity about life kept him going during his illness. Although he was suffering, Roland smiled a lot and his eyes twinkled.

In the middle of our exhibition preparatory work, I found one day that my hand was all swollen. I had not a clue as to how that had happened. I had no awareness of having been stung by an insect and I had not cut my finger and let it go septic. My hand was not throbbing but nevertheless was swelling more and more in a most alarming way! Since I was not registered with any doctor in Paris, I asked Roland if he would be kind enough to examine me, without making a fuss. He examined my hand and straightaway concluded that without my knowing it I had been bitten, probably by a spider. He handed me a prescription and I went straight to the chemist's behind the big department store called the Bazar de l'Hôtel de Ville.

Instead of an anti-inflammatory cream, Roland had prescribed me suppositories. Back home, I read the instructions for use on the box and was very taken aback. I did not know about this common practice in France at the time of taking medicines in the form of suppositories. I followed the instructions to the letter but could not let this unusual occurrence pass without making a comment about it later to Roland.

"It is much more effective that way, tu sais."

We were already on familiar terms.

"The medication goes straight into your bloodstream without having to go through your digestive system."

How right he was. The swelling soon went down without any side effects on the stomach.

One evening the Genots invited me to dinner in their flat in the sixteenth district. I think that the Iwayas were there also. When dinner was over, Roland brought out some of his photograph albums from the war. I half expected to see pictures of a very young French officer in his uniform, possibly group shots of young men full of team spirit, most probably against a military background. The albums were full of black-and-white photos stuck down in the usual way in rows, some of them captioned, but instead of smiling faces there were photos of prisoners in a concentration camp, page after page of people who were nothing more than skin and bone, and in amongst them there were some living skeletons who seemed to be trying at any price to pose before the camera with an element of dignity. Roland went on to explain. At the very end of the war, he had been seconded to the American army and sent as a young doctor to Buchenwald to carry out a medical examination of the French prisoners and determine which of them would be able to survive the journey back to France. The fate of the others was less clear. Too incapacitated to undergo this journey, they must have been cared for in the camp in appalling conditions and facing extreme shortages. What strength of mind he must have had to face up to such impossible decisions? What a heart-breaking way to embark on a career in medicine!

April came and I learnt that Cambridge University Press was offering me a job at its London branch. I was thrilled by this news, for at long last I saw a way forward for me in the world of publishing, something that I had always been drawn to. I told Marie-Louise all about what I was going to do, at the same time assuring her that I would not drop our plans for an exhibition. After all, it would be handy to be in London to finish off the British side of the exhibition.

In truth, the exhibition was bound to benefit hugely from my removal to London in October, but at the same time, the transition from a somewhat Bohemian lifestyle in Paris to that of a young executive in London was made easier by the work still to be done for the Paris show. The culture shock nonetheless was colossal.

44.
Clive on horseback in the Camargue

Towards the end of June, Peter dropped me a line. He wrote to say how much he had enjoyed our trip to the south of France in May and since our French year was nearing its end, suggested we should go back across there one last time. On our previous trip, I seem to remember, he had spoken about a novel he had been reading called *Caravan to Vaccarès* by Alistair Maclean, and I understood there and then that he had been taken by that writer's description of Arles and the Camargue. This aroused my curiosity to see these places for myself.

So here we were off once again, heading east in his reliable old car. We skirted the towns of Béziers, Montpellier and Nîmes. But on this July trip the weather was noticeably warmer than it had been in May. The sky had turned a dazzling blue and the cicadas up in the boughs of the olive trees kept up a rasping concert the whole length of our journey.

Straight after Nîmes, we headed towards Arles, where we soon checked into a two-star hotel. Next morning, we were in no great hurry and took a walk through the heart of this ancient town. We reached the Roman arena, a stone edifice awe-inspiring in its scale and antiquity. My mind wandered: I conjured up scenes of bloodshed as gladiators fought, and in the deep shadows of the arches it was easy to imagine that supernatural beings were lurking.

Back on the road to the Camargue! Before long we were

driving through a marshy landscape dotted with large brine lagoons even though we were quite far from the sea. Standing almost motionless in among the reeds were hundreds of pink flamingos. In the fields on either side of the road stood herds of Camargue bulls. With their long horns, lean build and brown coats, they were considerably less stocky than the black Spanish bulls such as I had seen in the Madrid bullring, but impressive all the same.

Every now and again, we spotted their herdsmen, riding grey Camargue horses. The tourist office in Arles had recommended that we paid a visit to the Paul Ricard ranch to go horse-riding along the paths by the lagoons. Wouldn't it be great to go riding with the herdsmen just as if we were young cowboys ourselves! It would not be my first time on horseback, for when I was about fourteen years old, I had had some riding lessons at Colchester Garrison Stables. There, my instructress, Mrs Sherwood, had once shouted out: "Mr Jackson, you are not riding in the Wild West now, you *sit* to the canter!"

By the time we reached the ranch and had found the stable we were itching to get on horseback, but there were three or four other tourists ahead of us waiting to go on the next ride. Half a dozen grey horses stood quietly, their reins looped around a hitching rail, their distinctive Spanish saddles looking as though they would be pretty comfortable and would afford a safe ride. With the help of a herdsman, all the visitors were mounted and off we went at a walking pace. The horses knew their way round the trail blindfold and soon sensed that their riders lacked equestrian skills. What a beautiful excursion it was: the air fragrant with the salt of the marshes, the lagoons nearby beckoning us to see the pink flamingos at closer quarters.

A hundred metres ahead, there was a fenced field full of bulls. All of a sudden, the herdsman spurred his horse into a canter. I got it into my head to leave Peter and the others behind and try and follow him and match his speed. Squeezing my heels against the horse's flanks, I set off at a canter. But foolishly I had reacted without having fully grasped the situation. The reason why the herdsman was in such a hurry soon became obvious. I saw that the gate into the field was half open and three bulls had split away from the herd and were standing there, scraping the ground with their hooves. The sight of those long and menacing horns was truly frightening, but all I could do was count on all my riding companion's experience to be able to defuse this dangerous situation. He uttered some firm commands to these bulls and two of them turned and filed back into the field. But the third one would not budge. He tossed his head, snorted, and began threatening us with his horns, all the while stamping the ground. It took the herdsman another two minutes before the bull turned tail and rejoined the herd.

Having made sure that the gate was properly shut, our courageous herdsman mopped his brow, and turning towards me with a stern look, said: "That could have been very dangerous for both of us, you know."

My rapid heartbeat echoed his sentiment. Peter and the others then caught up with us eager to know what had happened.

45.
John the balloon man

"By the way, Maryse," I blurted out from my desk in the translation department at the bank, "Is there a commercial directory I could have a quick look at?"

"Yes, there is, there's even one in this office."

Maryse could not contain her curiosity. "What do you need that for?"

"I want to find a balloon maker in the Paris area!" I answered, "A small factory where they make inflatable rubber balloons."

Maryse was not satisfied with my reply.

"Do you need that to do a translation?" she asked.

"Oh no, nothing like that, it's a private matter. If you give me the book, I'll tell you all about it."

Maryse came back from the cupboard where the dictionaries were kept clutching the book and said, "Right then, tell me what you are planning to do."

"All right then. Well, Chuchi, the Turkish friend I share my flat with, knows a Persian guy who earns his living by selling balloons in the park at Vincennes. Chuchi's idea is that we should do the same thing in the heart of Paris in the Tuileries Gardens."

"But you have a job here at the bank. I know it's only a temporary post, but all the same!"

"What we have got in mind is to sell balloons in the Tuileries at weekends to make enough money to throw parties."

The way the directory was laid out enabled me to find almost at once a list of balloon makers in France. And there, in the middle of the list, a Parisian address caught my eye. I can no longer quite remember the address, but it was near the Métro station at the Mairie de Montreuil. During the lunch break, having partaken of a hot meal served by Ali in the canteen, I set off towards the balloon maker's.

The way I remember it, it was not so much a factory, but rather an early twentieth-century gabled building in coloured bricks and dressed stone. The girl at the reception desk together with a colleague courteously showed me the range of balloons. There were small ones which blew up to the size of a football, undoubtedly meant for decorating rooms. There were bigger ones as broad as your shoulders. And there were even bigger ones, behind which you could almost hide yourself completely.

"For selling in parks, what I would suggest are the medium-sized ones. They come in bags of one hundred and cost fifty francs a bag, in other words, fifty centimes each."

"That's fine. I'll buy two bags."

"What are you going to fill them with? Helium? Air?"

"Air I think," I replied. "It's much easier and the balloons don't fly away so quickly if you let go of the string."

"Have you got a pump?"

"Oh. No!"

"Don't even think about blowing them up with your mouth. You'll wreck your lungs!"

"All right then. I need a pump as well. Would you mind showing me one please?"

The assistant came straight back with a pump which was simply designed but would do the job. You pressed up and down on the pump with your foot and air was forced into the balloon through a long rubber tube.

"And by the way, have you got a belt with pouches for the cash and to hold the balloons you are going to blow up?"

I left the factory with everything I needed to become a professional balloon seller and went back to the bank for all the world like a young executive after his midday stroll.

At long last the weekend came and Chuchi, his Swedish girlfriend and I set off from the Saint-Paul Métro station with a bag of medium-sized balloons, two belts with pouches, some small change, and a good bundle of lengths of string.

We pitched up at the main gate into the garden on the rue de Rivoli side, not far from the entrance to the Tuileries Métro station. And soon we began pumping, balloon after balloon. It was not long before we were completely surrounded by great brightly coloured orbs that shone in the sunlight, and at the slightest puff of wind tugged on the strings fastened to our belts just like a pack of hunting dogs on the leash.

"How much are your balloons?" inquired the passers-by.

"Two francs fifty," we answered.

Sales began to take off. One sale led to another. Children began shouting out loudly and repeatedly:

"Maman, je veux un ballon. I want a balloon, Mummy . . . Mummy, I want a balloon . . . !"

And those mothers worn down by hearing their children's shouts, soon gave in and bought lots of them.

"Don't you fill them with helium?" was a frequent remark.

"Oh no, only the polluted air of Paris. Like that, the balloons don't fly away so easily."

In the middle of the afternoon, one of the owners of the stalls erected inside the garden came over to us. He had a face like thunder.

"I know full well that you have not got a permit to sell balloons round here. So, what you are doing is totally illegal and what's more you are wrecking the market for our balloons. How on earth do you think that I can sell my balloons when you have the gall to stand there at the gate selling yours?"

I glanced quickly at his stall over in the shadow of the trees. It was true, he did sell balloons, I could see them hanging there, but they were pitifully small, only in pink and white and of very thin rubber. Nobody was taking the slightest interest in them – least of all any children.

"But actually, we are not in the gardens," I said politely. "We are selling our balloons at the gate."

"You have no right to do so, sir," he grumbled on. "As I have already said, you are breaking the law working like that. Vous faites la vente à la sauvette!"

Was he right in fact? Even if we were peddling without a permit, were we going to let this bully's outburst halt our business?

Our sales were getting better and better. While Jacqueline from Switzerland was in town, she loved spending an afternoon with us selling balloons. She took one home to Vevey, so she told me, and hung it from the ceiling in her mother's flat. The money was coming in thick and fast. Our takings on Bastille Day were the best yet, rising almost like a hot-air balloon; though in truth, they were still quite modest. Yet, we had embarked upon a good business and had earned enough to fund a few parties.

From our tentative beginnings at the garden gate on the rue de Rivoli, we grew our sales further by positioning ourselves at the main gates on the place de la Concorde. We grew our balloons as well, by buying the biggest and selling them alongside the medium-sized ones.

On one occasion, when I was back in Paris for a few days, I "requisitioned" a whole international team of friends. There was Sandra from Florence, Georges from Toulouse and Patrick from Dublin to cover the main entrances, including the one on the riverside. They were instructed to accept any currency in payment, especially the Deutschmark and the yen.

"And if someone from the office recognized me, I would be covered in embarrassment," said Patrick, who was already installed as a young executive at his Paris-based computer firm.

So, it was on one fine Sunday that I pitched up at the main gates on the place de la Concorde, with my team at the other gates. Parents were quick to pull out their purses to shut their children up, and behind me stretching the whole length of the garden there were soon bright blobs of colour waving and floating in the sun. Pierre-Auguste Renoir should have been there with his easel.

"Excusez-moi, Monsieur."

I turned around.

"Excusez-moi, Monsieur." And then in English: "May I take your photograph?"

A young American tourist was waving his camera around to show that he just had to take a shot which would sum up his impression of Paris: the seller of colourful balloons with the Champs-Élysées and the Arc de Triomphe in the background.

"By all means!"

"Here is a franc. Thank you, sir!"

Later that same afternoon, all the West African street sellers, who like me were selling a few steps away from the gates on the place de la Concorde, suddenly started to bundle into big holdalls their wooden knick-knacks and their handbags made from exotic skins, and then to roll up their straw mats.

"I wonder what is going on," I asked myself.

But all the Africans had already skedaddled, and I was left standing there laden with a bunch of big and medium-sized inflated balloons.

A police van swept into the service road just outside the gates. There was only me left to deal with the police who were coming towards me. I was well and truly frozen to the spot.

The police van stopped right in front of me. My heart missed a beat. There was no disguising the fact that I was selling balloons without a licence. There were no excuses; there was no way round it: at the very least there would be a cross-examination down at the police station.

A small, barred window in the left side of the vehicle opened. A policeman, who seemed quite friendly, stuck his head out and spoke to me:

"How much are your balloons?"

"Um, two francs fifty for a medium-sized one and, um, ten francs for a big one."

"OK, I'll buy two of the big ones. My children will just love those big balloons. Don't bother blowing them up. They wouldn't go through the window."

"Fair enough," I replied. "I'll knock something off the price for you: let's say, sixteen francs for the two of them."

"Many thanks, young fellow, and happy selling!"

The barred window closed, and the police van rumbled off.

"Goodbye and thank you very much!" I sighed.

46.
Clive wields his knife and fork at Les Baux-de-Provence

Having survived our horse-riding adventure Peter next consulted his guidebook to see which other nearby places might be worth a visit. After a few minutes' perusal he singled out a place called Les Baux-de-Provence, the guidebook describing it as a very attractive hilltop village, and one which was also home to a well-regarded restaurant and hotel.

It was mid-afternoon when we set off for the village and after an hour's drive we were there. We parked the car in a large square and on foot followed a road up a steep hill, which took us to the heights of the village. A panoramic view of sun-drenched countryside and rolling hills unfurled before our eyes. We wandered around the narrow streets exploring every nook and cranny before traipsing back down to the car as the church clock struck seven. It was time to try out the restaurant, which was called L'Ostaù de Baumanière.

The only immediate snag was this: having checked out of our hotel in Arles early that morning and gone horse-riding in the Camargue, we were still wearing our jeans and T-shirts. We climbed in the car and made our way to the edge of the village, where a sign heralded the presence of our restaurant, a fine white building surrounded by a wall broken only by the entrance to its car park. Peter steered our humble Simca into the courtyard and gingerly eased it in between two sleek limousines just as an elegant gentleman in livery hurried toward us and opened the car door for Peter. At that moment it suddenly dawned on us that L'Ostaù might well have been the preserve of high society. But now was hardly the right moment to give up on our culinary mission. We climbed out of the car with all the self-confidence we could muster.

As our liveried gentleman ushered us towards the restaurant, we felt even more aware of our rough-and-ready attire. We skirted a most beautiful terrace laid out with tables and fringed with olive trees, in the middle of which a fountain played. Seated at one of the terrace tables we spotted an immaculately well-dressed elderly man who was dining alone. He was wearing a suit which had that unmistakable cut of a Savile Row tailor. When he overheard us conversing in English, he put down his fork, raised his head and shot a rather equivocal look in our direction. In a flash I had got it: I had made the connection between the beautiful Rolls-Royce I had seen in the car park and the face of the man in front of us. And I could see that Peter had come to the same realization. We both felt we knew who he was. Wasn't this gentleman the celebrated playwright Noël Coward?

When we went into the restaurant building, one of the waiters came over to greet us and discreetly led us to a table half hidden away behind one of the arches. While the waiter may not have approved of our dress, his expression betrayed no sign of it. On the other hand, some of the other diners could barely hide their disapproval. The well-heeled American family sitting at the next table was somewhat aghast as we sat down. However, their son, who looked about sixteen, smiled at us and said "Hi". But a stern warning from his father, who said, "Don't talk to those people," must have made him think that we were about as socially acceptable as lepers.

At a table away to our right there was a couple clearly relishing their dinner. The man, who looked about forty-five, was wearing a flashy jacket and a bright yellow silk tie. His dining companion, a young blond-haired lady, wore a fine green dress, perhaps haute-couture, and an overwhelming perfume that wafted through the whole restaurant. Although her likely age was no more than twenty-five, she could have been his wife, but more likely not. They both kept shooting scornful and irritated looks in our direction.

Well-groomed though this lady was, she was no match for the natural beauty of Marianne.

The restaurant staff could not have behaved more impeccably towards us. After having pored over the mouth-watering offerings on the menu, but nervous about running up a big bill, we skipped the first course and chose the leg of lamb served with green beans. Next came the moment to choose the wine from the list brought to us by the leather-aproned wine steward. Taking his considered advice, we chose the red wine from the vineyards belonging to the restaurant itself. The leg of lamb was brought to our table on a trolley, and we watched attentively as the waiter deftly carved the tender meat and balanced each slice on the flat of the blade before placing it on our plates. As for the wine, to our unsophisticated palate, we thought it was up there among the Rhône region's best.

Peter quietly put down his knife and fork and, leaning over towards me with a broad grin on his face, said, "Guess what, I have just overheard our American friends telling the waiter to bring them exactly what we're eating!"

To round off the meal a vast array of cheeses was wheeled to our table on an enormous tray. We spotted one or two cheeses that we readily recognized, but there were many others: some wrapped in vine leaves; others coated with ground pepper; some in slices; some in whole rounds. We had never seen some of them before. Where should we begin? We politely pointed at the ones that looked most appealing, at the same time asking the waiter to tell us what they were called and where they came from.

We had an inkling that the staff had perhaps needed to revise their opinion of these two young Englishmen in their inappropriate clothes. When all was said and done, we spoke pretty good French with them, and we did know our table manners. Besides, it was not unheard of for eccentric English aristocrats to turn up at the finest eateries in France wearing the wrong attire. It only remains to be said that our dinner at L'Ostaù was beyond reproach: the greatest culinary experience we had ever had. However, we could not help but think that the manager breathed a sigh of relief as we drove off.

A few years later, we were delighted to learn in the British press that Her Majesty Queen Elizabeth had stayed at L'Ostaù de Baumanière while on an official visit to France. So, there you are. Our preliminary inspection must have brought immeasurable success to this establishment! Peter has hung onto the bill from the feast we had so much enjoyed in that illustrious restaurant.

Back at Salies it felt as though I was coming back to earth with a bump. Dining at L'Ostaù, we had savoured a most wonderful meal. But this set me thinking about how little time was left to me here in France before going back to face the stifling regime of lectures and essay-writing at college in London this coming autumn.

René was well aware of how attached I had become to the French way of life and all its charms, and so, the evening before I left Salies for good, he had organized a farewell party for me over at the café in Carresse.

There they all were: many of my colleagues from the school had turned out to say goodbye. And there was Monsieur Camy standing behind the bar as usual wearing his blue dungarees and solemn expression. He did manage a smile as he shook my hand and wished me all the best. And his daughters Josiane and Evelyne darted out from behind the bar to snatch a quick farewell kiss.

"Now, don't start thinking that England is going to beat France again in the Five Nations Rugby Championship next year!" said Marcel Saule as he raised a glass of wine to me.

Joseph, who was standing next to me, added: "We're sorry to see you go. We never thought we'd ever get on so well with one of those perfidious Englishmen. You've really become one of us."

Next morning, René, Joseph and Jean-Baptiste were standing with me outside the main house at Mosquéros as I waited for the taxi to come. René was in usual top form, teasing me mercilessly, saying that I would certainly miss all their fine south-western French food and wine, not to mention the sunny climate of the Béarn now that I was returning to a land of rain and fog.

"Au revoir, Clive. Bonne chance pour l'avenir. Nous ne t'oublierons jamais! We'll never forget you!"

The fading sound of their voices followed the taxi as it moved off along the driveway.

47.
John's private view

David Marsden, sales representative for Merlin, a printer on Canvey Island in Essex, had done his stuff. A big brown-paper parcel of posters for the exhibition had been delivered to my office at Cambridge University Press on the Euston Road in London. There was another much smaller parcel with it. Inside were the invitation cards.

Yes, I could see right away that David had done a good job. Stuck on the outside of the parcel of posters there was a copy to show what was inside. Anyway, I opened the package and drew out a pristine poster.

"Ah! That's perfect," I said to myself. "That's exactly what I needed."

I had taken on the role of organizer and had commissioned Quentin Blake to do us an attractive poster drawing. He had done a cartoon sketch in pencil of a figure of a man laden with drawings and had surrounded it with wording written in his highly attractive and eccentric style printed in red.

I undid one end of the smaller package to take out an invitation done on the habitual yellow card of the Galerie Genot. On it were printed the names of the French and British artists. It was altogether quite an impressive list of humorous artists from both sides of the Channel. I was beginning to dream how successful the show was likely to be.

Unfortunately, the business of French customs had not entered my head. There I was at Orly airport, some days later, being questioned by a stern customs officer.

"Well, sir, you are importing publicity material," he said, eyeing the invoice I had given him. "There is VAT payable, and on top of that import duty."

I only had the vaguest notion of what value-added tax meant. This had only been imposed in the United Kingdom since the previous year; unlike in France, where every citizen had long been taxed on their every business transaction.

"But, Monsieur, it's only a small number of posters and invitations for a small exhibition being held in Paris."

"Yes, so I see. And why did you have this printed in England?"

"Er, well, I commissioned an English artist to do the drawing for the poster and so it was easier to have everything printed in England."

"Very well then. Given that the quantity is so small, I am going to let it go through on this occasion. But next time you must not forget the VAT."

*

At long last, the day of the private view had arrived. In the vaulted room downstairs a selection of the best drawings had been hung on the walls, but it was quite a job to see them because of the crush. Piem and Desclozeaux were there in person, representing the French side and Quentin Blake and my father the British. Henry Meyric Hughes from the British Council was also there. Toru and Keiko Iwaya came along, as did Georges Casas and Patrick Currivan, not to forget my friend Lorraine from Northamptonshire, my mother and brother. What a jolly occasion it was – and the pictures were selling.

All of a sudden, the entrance door opened and in walked a small middle-aged woman. She seemed to be slightly tipsy. Marie-

Louise spotted her.

"Oh, do let her in," she said to me. "She doesn't have an invitation, but that doesn't matter."

"But who is it?" I whispered.

"It's Jeanne, Modigliani's daughter."

In truth, I had already seen her from time to time wandering the streets of the Marais, without knowing who she was. I learnt from Marie-Louise that she led a somewhat sad and lonely life but loved to attend private views.

By way of celebrating the opening of the show, Marie-Louise invited my parents, my brother and me along with Huguette and Roland for dinner at the restaurant Chez Robert one or two days later. That evening, there was a distinctly odd feeling in the air, for Robert for some reason was out of sorts. As he stood before the fire at the back of the room, turning the beef steaks in the flames, he was grumbling under his breath. Nobody understood why. His wife, a tiny slip of a woman in her printed calico smock and huge apron, served us attentively with liver pâté garnished with a lettuce leaf and, to drink, jugs of red wine. Robert came over to our table in his blue-striped apron and in a temper to serve our steaks.

"But I'm fed up to the teeth with all this: *merde, merde alors*."

My mother turned to Marie-Louise and in perfect French quietly asked her:

"What *does* he mean by that?"

Epilogue

The motion of the breaking waves on the shore altered and instinctively Clive knew that the tide was turning.

"Time we were heading for dry land," he said.

John still had his head full of the Paris opening and did not hear him.

"And time we went and had a bite to eat," Clive suggested with growing urgency in his voice. "Do you fancy some seafood at the Company Shed?"

This immediately brought John out of his daydreaming and, brushing the salt off his arms, he replied:

"Great idea. Seafood would be perfect!"

The Company Shed was down on West Mersea harbour. You could not have found a less pretentious restaurant anywhere. On arrival, John paused a moment, his eyes running down the wide choice of dishes chalked up on the blackboard outside.

Clive nudged open the door.

"Let's see if they have a couple of seats for us."

John was struck by the huge variety of people sitting around the large communal tables. He spotted the day trippers straight-away; some certainly had London accents. There were also locals, as well as dedicated fish-lovers who had come from far and wide to savour the seafood. The ages of the guests were just as varied.

To the left, was the fresh-fish counter with heaps of fish sitting on mounds of ice. Behind that was the kitchen, where some of the staff were busy shucking oysters and dressing crabs.

A waitress came over to us.

"I have booked a couple of seats for Jackson," Clive announced.

Vacant seats were found among the din of the diners. As they squeezed themselves onto their seats, John felt almost as squashed as if he were sitting shoulder to shoulder with fellow gourmets in a Parisian brasserie.

The door at the back of the premises opened and in strode an impressively tall man with clear-blue eyes. He was wearing overalls and wellington boots, the uniform of a man from a long line of fishermen and oyster breeders. He spotted Clive right away and came over smiling to the table.

"Good to see you here again, Clive," he said.

"This is Richard Haward," said Clive to John, "we were at school together."

"A very long time ago," Richard interjected, with a twinkle in his eye.

Clive had clearly planned everything ahead, for he brought out a cool bag from the depths of his rucksack, opened it and plonking a bottle of Macon-Villages and some bread and butter on the table said: "This restaurant provides the seafood dishes, but you are always welcome to bring along your own wine if you don't want to order one of the house wines."

John was beginning to think that any similarity with a brasserie was about to come to an end when Clive ordered a large seafood platter for two and, to start with, a plate of oysters. Before you could say Company Shed, the two men had set to eating. After the large juicy oysters came the platter on which was heaped a huge mound of crab, crayfish, prawns, cockles, mussels, as well as smoked salmon and mackerel.

"You really would think that we were still in France," John had to admit, as he cracked open a juicy crab claw. "Here we are reliving some of those great culinary times!"

"But how lucky we were to have had all those experiences back then!" added Clive.

"You know, living in France, was such a great adventure and an enriching journey for us," said John.

"And all the more so when you look back from the present day."

Clive broke open a crayfish and dug the prongs of his fork into it.

"And coming back to England at that time . . ." he went on.

"Ah, I remember all of that," answered John. "What a shock! England then was in such a sorry state. Remember? The miners' strikes, the financial crisis, the power cuts!"

"Yes. There seemed an overwhelming sense of hardship wherever you looked."

"Whereas in France things seemed to be soaring, to be on the up and up."

John began thinking about his own return to England. He remembered feeling that it was as if he had taken the wrong turning and that he should have gone straight back to Paris, where the bank had been trying to entice him with the offer of a permanent job. Even the contrast between the dreary Underground station of Euston Square near his London office and the brighter Métro station of Filles du Calvaire, a short walk from his old Paris flat, had been enough to make him yearn for the City of Light.

"We had a rather rose-tinted vision of the country, didn't we?" he said. "Yet historic upheavals also affected France; before, during and after our time there, but, somehow or other, we didn't really take that on board when we were there."

"What exactly do you mean by that?" asked Clive.

"Well, there were problems in France as elsewhere, but they only really impinged on us when they affected our friends and acquaintances."

Yes, but there had indeed been glimpses of a troubled France in the days of their youth: the hostile glances of Parisians in the street directed at harmless film extras clad in the uniform of the Compagnies républicaines de sécurité who were mistaken for the ruthless suppressors of the riots of '68; Marianne earnestly expressing her envy of Britain as a land of free health care and good social-housing provision; and the aftermath of a war with Algeria which had uprooted Maurice and so many others from the land of their birth.

There was a lull in their conversation and for a while the two men finished off the seafood platter without speaking.

The time had come for them to leave the Company Shed and they strolled back to the beach. There, their French dream gave way to English reality with a jolt. It was low tide now and the estuary waters had retreated to a far-off channel. The swimming platforms lay lifeless on the mud.

At a cable's length from the shore an oystercatcher skimmed a shingle bank, shrieking against the stillness.

Silhouette of John Adamson by an unknown street artist, Tuileries Gardens, Paris, August 1969.

Acknowledgements

This book began its life written by us in French with a working title of *Perfidie et douceur*. While we lived in France the language we heard all around us left a deep impression on us and on our memories. When we translated the draft text, we hoped to retain more of a French ambience than writing our stories directly in English would have given us.

Most, perhaps ninety-five per cent or more, of what we wrote is based on fact and on memory. All the rest is invention – or lapse of memory. Most names, however, are indeed those of the people we met.

We owe a debt of gratitude to Meg Jackson, Peter Adamson and Sophie Rixon as well as to the late Jacques Beauroy for critically reading our prose and making invaluable suggestions, and to Chris Jones for her elegant layout of the book.

Norfolk Summer: Making *The Go-Between*

CHRISTOPHER HARTOP

Joseph Losey's award-winning movie *The Go-Between* was filmed entirely on location in Norfolk in 1970. The film charts the tragic story of a young boy's loss of innocence during a hot summer and stars Julie Christie and Alan Bates as a pair of lovers crossing class boundaries in late Victorian England. The production brought together the playwright Harold Pinter, who adapted L. P. Hartley's elegant novel for the screen, the acclaimed director Joseph Losey and a cast of international stars for ten weeks' filming in and around Melton Constable Hall in north Norfolk – a time of happy creativity, some tension and a good deal of comedy. But the idyllic summer only came about after years of bitter battling over the rights of the book, and it was to be followed by yet more intrigue and high drama, which culminated in the film's triumph at the 1971 Cannes Film Festival, where it won the prestigious Palme d'Or.

"Charming and generously illustrated" *The Spectator*

Paperback: 978-1-898565-07-9
norfolksummer.co.uk

A

John Adamson
johnadamsonbooks.com